MEDIEVAL WARFARE

Here is a fascinating study of the history of warfare during the nine centuries from A.D. 600 to 1500. Although the author concentrates mainly upon developments in Western Europe, he looks, too, beyond these frontiers at the military machine of the Byzantine Empire, the terrible armies of Genghis Khan and Mahomet, and the heroic battles of the Crusaders. Tracing the development of tactics from early Byzantine practice, the author develops the story through the rise of feudal cavalry, which dominated European battlefields until its decline and ultimate supercession by infantrymen, and by the artillery of the fifteenth century.

A study of war can often be highly revealing, not only of political history, but of the whole evolution of human society and of human attitudes, and the author of the present volume does not lose sight of the fact that war is essentially about people. What for example did men of the Middle Ages mean by a "just war"? What was the influence upon the conduct of war of religion and chivalry on one hand, or material gain on another? How far were ordinary people caught up in the horrors of war? In seeking answers to these and other questions, the author has drawn upon a wide range of contemporary graphic material, much of which may be unfamiliar to modern students. It is therefore hoped that in this addition to the WAYLAND PICTORIAL SOURCES SERIES the reader will not only acquire a practical grasp of the technical side of medieval warfare—weapons, armour, castles, transport, organization and command—but will acquire a deeper understanding of the quality of life in those centuries loosely termed the Middle Ages.

A WAYLAND PICTORIAL SOURCES BOOK

MEDIEVAL WARFARE

GEOFFREY HINDLEY

WAYLAND PUBLISHERS LONDON

The Wayland Pictorial Sources Series

The Voyages of Discovery   G. R. CRONE AND A. KENDALL
The Medieval Establishment   GEOFFREY HINDLEY
The French Revolution   DOUGLAS JOHNSON
Shakespeare's England   LEVI FOX
The American Revolution   ROGER PARKINSON
The Dawn of Man   VINCENT MEGAW AND RHYS JONES
Twentieth Century China   JOHN ROBOTTOM
The Russian Revolution   LIONEL KOCHAN
The American Civil War   KEITH ELLIS

Frontispiece: French miniaturist's impression of the siege
of a castle (from the fifteenth century *Roman de la Rose*)

Copyright © 1971 by Wayland Publishers Ltd
101 Grays Inn Road, London, WC1
SBN 85340 030 X

Printed in Great Britain by Jarrold and Sons Ltd, Norwich

CONTENTS

TABLE OF EVENTS

CHAPTER ONE
THE HEIRS OF ROME

THE OUTSTANDING DEVELOPMENT between the warfare of the Roman Empire and that of Medieval Europe was the evolution of heavy feudal cavalry in the early eighth century. In Roman times, infantry manœuvres had lain at the centre of operations. The cavalry had been used in support, as skirmishers, and to turn an enemy retreat into a rout. After the age of Charlemagne (742–814), the mounted warrior was the all-important figure in European warfare, and the infantry were generally despised. Between the collapse of Rome in the fifth century and the rise of this new type of mounted warfare, European battles seem to have been unscientific affairs— disorganized skirmishes in which numbers and morale counted for more than skilled generalship.

In the Eastern Roman Empire, however, military techniques evolved in an unbroken tradition from the days of the Ancient Empire. The Empire's centre of gravity shifted to Constantinople, founded as Rome's twin capital early in the fourth century. For a thousand years, the emperors who ruled from this great city maintained a powerful Christian state in the Balkans, and in the territory now occupied by modern Turkey. The Byzantines—named after Byzantium, the ancient Greek city that provided Constantinople's site—were a Middle Eastern people of mixed racial origins. They were to use Greek as the official language, and under Constantine the Great (306–37) had adopted Christianity as the state religion. Yet their rulers could trace their authority back through an unbroken line to the old Roman Empire of Augustus. They regarded themselves as Romans, and the defenders of the Roman Empire.

In Europe, the barbarian successor kingdoms to Rome fought among themselves to control the rich imperial inheritance, or simply to make good dubious claims to petty territorial ambitions. The Rome of the East, however, rightly saw itself as the defender of civilization. The object was survival, and the defeat of the numerous and recurring waves of enemies which pounded upon the eastern frontiers from the steppes of Asia, from the great and equally venerable Empire of Persia, and the nomads of Arabia. The rival gangs of Europe's petty princelings battled in a common tradition of warfare; they knew one another's tactics because they all used the same. In such a situation victory went to the strong and the brave. But at Constantinople, war became an object of scientific study. The imperial generals observed the tactics of Turk, Saracen, Persian and Slav enemies, and adapted their own tactics to deal with them. For centuries, too, the Byzantines ruled provinces in Italy; here they came into contact with the Lombards, and later with the heavy mounted troops of the feudal host. The Byzantines did not despise the bravery of the northern European warriors. Nor did they underestimate the immense damage that a properly delivered charge of these armoured specialists could inflict upon an ill-prepared army. But they were frankly astonished by the cavalier attitude of the Westerners to the business of warfare. In the East, war had for centuries been a grim and serious affair; enslavement and destruction were the penalties of defeat. In the West, where except for brief periods the enemy was internal rather than external, the consequences were not so weighty. Byzantine defeats at the hands of the Arabs during the seventh century led to the serious losses of the rich provinces of Syria and Egypt for ever. Alexandria, one of the patriarchates of the Eastern Church, was captured for Islam in 642. When failure could cost so much, victory by any means mattered far more than romantic displays of chivalry.

It has been estimated that during the sixth century the Emperor Justinian (527–65) maintained a standing army of 150,000, drawn from a population of only five millions. The Byzantine state was indeed geared to war. The major part of its forces were stationed at garrisons on the frontiers and in towns in the interior. Under Justinian, and for a hundred years longer, most of the troops were barbarians recruited from beyond the frontiers. This system continued the practice of the later Roman Empire. In the West, these barbarians were recruited in large units under their own Gothic commanders. Eastern Rome on the other hand, took care to enlist their potentially dangerous allies as individuals serving under Byzantine commanders.

In the early seventh century, the Byzantine army was radically reorganized. Indeed, the change seems to have nearly caused a social revolution in the Empire. The heart of Byzantium's strength was the wide upland plain of Anatolia (Turkey). This was restructured into large *themes* (military districts) each commanded by a *strategos* (military official). The *strategos* had a civilian proconsul as his second-in-command. Large landed estates formerly owned by great men were broken up and the land used to settle peasant smallholders, in return for obligatory service. To settle the *themes*, troops were withdrawn from former frontier posts, and even the crack troops of the Empire were integrated into this "farmers' militia." At the end of the seventh century, Slav war prisoners were forcibly settled in Anatolia and the result was the growth of a virtual citizens' army. The soldiers of Byzantium were no longer barbarians of uncertain allegiance; they were land-holding citizens of the state, who were expected to arm and mount themselves from the proceeds of their farms. The system produced a flexible and efficient army and navy; the *theme* on the southern coast of Anatolia was responsible for providing sailors.

Light and heavy cavalry both played an important part in Byzantine tactics. From the eighth century, the heavy cavalry was improved by the adoption of details of armour and harness learned from the Frankish West. But if mounted troops always played a major role in Byzantine war, they were but only one element in a versatile war machine. They never came to dominate it at the expense of the infantry, as happened in the West. The general of the armies of Eastern Rome commanded a force with varied capabilities, and it was his task to deploy this force as efficiently as possible, according to the science of war.

For a thousand years, Constantinople was one of the magic cities of world history (1). The proud heritage of Rome was transmuted by the riches of the eastern trade routes. From Persia, India and even distant China, merchandise—gold, jewels, textiles and spices—flooded into the superb natural harbour formed by the inlet behind the promontory on which the city stood. The Byzantines called it the Golden Horn. In time of war, a chain boom was raised across its entrance to keep out enemy ships. On the landward side, stood the massive fortifications begun by Emperor Theodosius II (408–50); they stood unbreached for a thousand years (2). Consisting of a triple wall defended at regular intervals by strong towers, the fortifications stretched for three miles across the isthmus. The site of Constantinople seemed to be designed by Nature herself as a defensive fortress. But throughout her

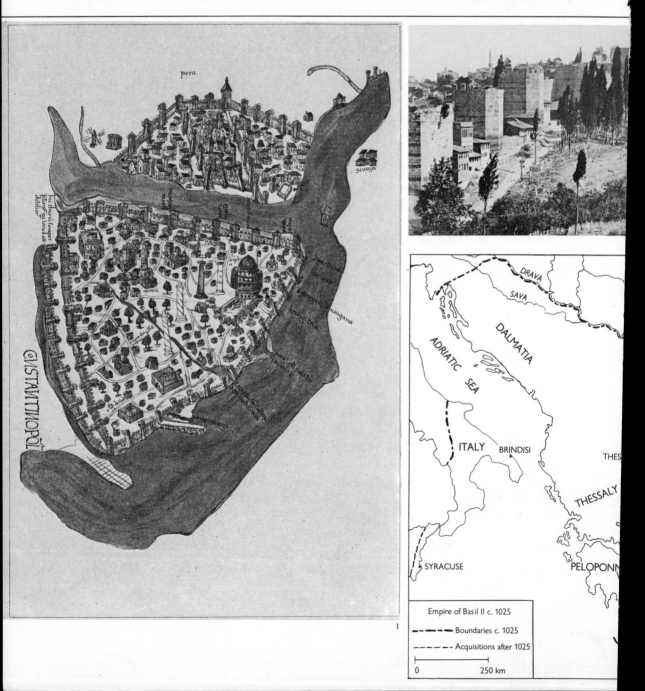

I

Empire of Basil II c. 1025

— · — · — Boundaries c. 1025

— — — — Acquisitions after 1025

0   250 km

long history, the Byzantine Empire often took the offensive against her enemies; the memory of her Roman past was long kept alive by her artists (3). At the start of the seventh century, the military machine that was to keep the Empire in being was re-established by Emperor Maurice (582–602) (4). Shortly after this, the improved army won a series of dazzling victories under Emperor Heraclius, who came to the throne in 610 (5). Yet when he died in 641, the Empire was once again on the defensive. Century after century, hostile waves of invaders beat on the frontiers. In the early eleventh century the Empire had made another comeback. The map (6) shows the frontiers in 1028 embracing modern Turkey, Greece, Bulgaria, Albania, parts of Yugoslavia and even Italy.

11

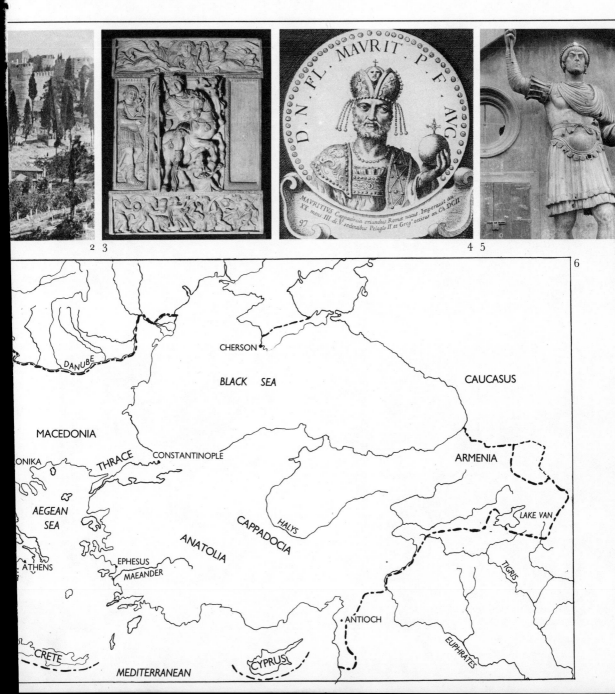

2 3

4 5

6

In her long history, Byzantium encountered many enemies, each with different tactics. First came the Persians (7), the heirs to a great Empire as old as Rome herself. After them came the fierce armies of the new faith of Islam (8). The light horsemen of Arabia and their allies made lightning conquests during the seventh century that threatened not only the Empire of Constantinople, but Western Europe, too, and which destroyed forever the Persian power already weakened by Heraclius. In 626, Constantinople withstood a siege by the wild horsemen of the Avar tribes from the central Eurasian steppe (9). At the end of the seventh century, Bulgar tribes from the Volga region crossed the River Danube and carved out an empire from lands formerly controlled by Byzantium. In the ninth century, the Bulgars were converted to Eastern Orthodox Christianity by missionaries from Constanti-

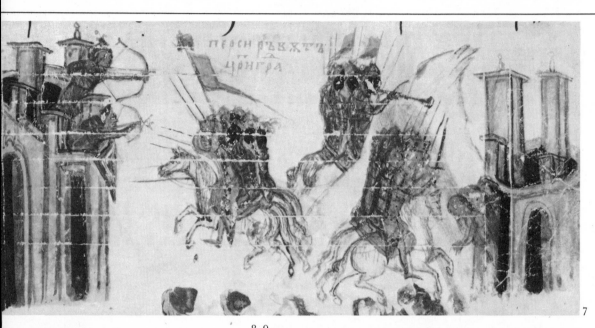

7

8 9

nople. But the Bulgar armies (10) remained the inveterate enemies of the Byzantines until they were savagely put down by the great Emperor Basil II (976–1025), nicknamed "the Bulgar-slayer." One of the heroes of Byzantine history, Basil pushed his frontiers to the Caucasus in the east and held the line against the Lombards (11) in Italy. His successors in the Italian provinces faced a new enemy in the Normans. Basil II's immediate predecessors

—John Tsimisces and Nicephorus Phocas (12)—had forced back the Arab dynasties on the eastern and southern frontiers. But after Basil's death, a period of internal weakness enabled the Seljuk Turks (who destroyed the old Arab regimes in Persia, Iraq and Syria) to infiltrate into Byzantine Anatolia. The following pages look at the techniques used by the Byzantines to meet these varied threats.

10

12

11

During ten centuries, Byzantium naturally suffered defeats as well as victories. But the Empire had a military system that was potentially strong, not only in men and materials, but in theoretical work, too. The military textbook unknown in the West until the late Middle Ages, was common in the East from an early period (13). Emperor Maurice wrote one in the 590s. The most famous Byzantine military textbook is the *Tactica* by Leo VI ("the Wise") written about 900. The field commander led a versatile force of heavy and light mounted brigades, and heavy and light infantry. The *kaballarios* (heavy trooper) wore a steel cap with a decorative crest, a long mail shirt, gauntlet and heavy shoes. In hot weather he would wear a surcoat as protection against the sun, in cold weather a cloak which was carried at the saddle. The heavy trooper's weapons were a sword, dagger and a long lance

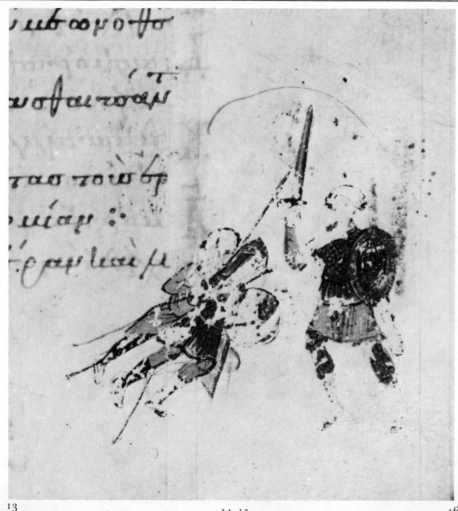

13

14 15

16

attached to the forearm by a thong. His horse, too, had head and neck armour. The light cavalry wore less armour, and carried only a lance, sword and shield (14, 15, 16). The *scutati* (heavy infantry) were protected by a crested helmet, waist-length mail shirt, and a large oblong shield bearing the regimental emblem. The infantry's chief weapons were battle-axe and dagger. The *psiloi* (light infantry) were primarily a missile force. Their heavy bows shot further than those of their own horsemen and enemy horsemen. Other troops in this infantry corps were armed with three or four light throwing-spears (17, 18). The *psiloi* had only a small round shield for defence, and if they were expecting hand-to-hand combat would also carry a battle-axe. The troops were recruited from the Anatolian peasant soldiery and the Armenian subjects of the Empire.

17

18

16 Byzantine armies were noted for their good discipline and organization. The largest fighting unit, the *bandon* of cavalry, had a maximum of 500 men. As most officers were appointed centrally the chain of command was effective down to the lowest units. Three *banda* made a *moirach*, and three *moirachs* a *meros* of about 3,000 men. This was the unit of march. The commander of the whole force, the *strategos*, was the senior officer (*merarch*). From the sixth century, the cavalry was the most important part of the army (19, 20), helping the great generals Belisarius and Narses to reconquer Africa and Italy for the Emperor Justinian the Great (527–65). Emperor Heraclius defeated the Persians in 627 in a great set battle (21).

The complex battle order of the later Empire was so designed that the army could withstand repeated attacks, and deliver many

19

20 21

counter-blows. The army often held the field for months at a time, supported by an auxiliary force directed by the *tuldophylax*, with medical staff paid by commission, grooms, waggoners and packhorses (22). Regular garrisons were housed in large stone castles, but since most of Byzantium's enemies were unfamiliar with siege warfare, these castles were often little more than walled camps (23). The Byzantines preferred to avoid hopeless battles, and were amazed by over-bold European commanders who neglected strategy. A good Byzantine general always kept his ears open for information from scouts or prisoners. If the enemy's position seemed too strong, the army might await a better chance, or enter negotiations after parleys had been initiated by heralds (24). In his *Tactics*, Leo VI explained how negotiators could trick an enemy, or lull him into a false sense of security (25).

22

23

24

25

The weapons used by Byzantine troops were those found in most contemporary armies (26, 27). The short bow, despite its size, had a respectable range of about 150 yards; and the other missile weapon, the sling, was familiar enough in the East though less common in Western Europe (28). But Byzantium was ahead of the West in its use of siege artillery, thanks to the living Roman tradition. The most famous weapon in the Byzantine arsenal was the mysterious "Greek fire." Possibly the first instance of the "secret" weapon in history, it was certainly the most successful: the secret was kept for centuries. Greek fire was first used at sea and was developed during the blockade of Constantinople by the Arab fleet that lasted from 673 to 677. In fact, the Arabs threatened the capital even longer than this. During the reign of Emperor Constantine IV (668–86) they controlled the strategic Sea of Marmora.

26

27

28

In this time of emergency the capital was thronged with refugees from all over the Empire. One of these, Kallinikos, a Greek from Syria, devised an explosive mixture believed to have contained sulphur, naphtha and quicklime. The mixture was projected from copper tubes and ignited on contact with the moist side of the enemy ships, or with the sea. In addition to the ordinary ships of the time (29, 30), the Byzantine fleet was soon fitted out with *siphonophores* (31). These were ships equipped with tubes or siphons for throwing the fire, and which were used to great effect in later campaigns. Eventually, various types of Greek fire were developed outside the Empire. Depictions of flame-throwing tubes in early manuscripts once led to suggestions that they were primitive cannons.

29

30

31

Islam's seventh-century triumphs in war led to much heart-searching in Eastern Christendom. The outcome shows the impact of military defeat on the psychology of a society. Most Byzantines felt their defeats were a judgement from God, and noticed that the Infidel did not use images in religious worship. Emperor Leo III (717–41), who repulsed the last Arab siege of the capital in 717–18, also forbade icon worship, and had images destroyed and overpainted (32). The triumphant reassertion of Byzantine power culminated in the conquests of Basil II, the Bulgar-slayer (33). But it lasted only half a century. The menace of the Seljuk Turks grew during the eleventh century, and in 1071 they defeated the Byzantine army at Manzikert on the eastern frontier. This historic disaster, in which Emperor Romanus IV was captured, was due to great treachery and a disregard for the

rules of Byzantine military theory. manus wished to force a great victory against the Turks. But having divided his army before his inefficient reconnaissance revealed the enemy, he fought from a position of his enemy's choosing. The Empire's military strength was slowly rebuilt by Alexius (d. 1118) (34), but in 1176 the army of Manuel I was cut to pieces at the battle of Myriocephalum as it tried to force a narrow pass against the Turks. The Emperor's senior advisers warned against entering the deep valley but were overruled. By ignoring its long tradition of professionalism, the imperial army went down catastrophically. The grand era of military history was over. The capture of Constantinople through the treachery of the Western knights of the Fourth Crusade in 1204 signed its epitaph (35, 36).

32

33

34

35

36

CHAPTER TWO
THE MATERIALS OF WAR

WHEN THE BYZANTINE ARMY was being developed as a model fighting force in the early seventh century, the armies of Western Europe were little more than armed mobs. They relied on weight, numbers and sheer physical courage for their victories. The western armies that fought beside the Byzantines during the First Crusade in 1097 were led by a hardy band of professional, highly specialized cavalry units. This cavalry represented an entirely new type of warfare.

The theme of this next chapter is the story of how a principle of warfare shaped a whole society. Here we shall deal with the development of weapons and the raw materials of war from the eighth century, when the mounted warrior came to dominate the battlefields of the West, to the close of the Middle Ages. During these seven centuries the heavily armoured horseman reached the peak of his military effectiveness, and then began to decline in the face of new techniques. In the process his armour became ever more elaborate, and reached a pinnacle of efficiency in the mid-fifteenth century, just when the knight was being rudely displaced from his position of honour in the battle order. The armourer was one of the most highly skilled and advanced technicians of medieval society. Indeed, the development of his craft, and of the essential science of metallurgy, forms part of the history of medieval technology. The constant aim of the armourer was to give

his client the greatest physical freedom to wield his weapons, and the best protection from those of his opponent. The uproar of the battlefield was echoed in the noise of the smithy, and the conflict of European knighthood reflected the competition between her swordsmiths and armourers. Today the competitive technology of war is all too familiar, but it is nothing new. We generally think of the Middle Ages as a stagnant period in the history of technical advance, but in the field of weaponry at least this is a mistaken impression. The feudal knight was a highly professional fighting man. His training began in boyhood and lasted into his late teens. Like any professional, he made himself expert in the tools of his trade and constantly looked about for improvements. Specialization intensified as the Middle Ages progressed, until the swordsmiths of Toledo and the armourers of Nuremberg and Milan won a European reputation.

Important advances were made in the design of missile weapons. The short bow, known since antiquity, was useless against the heavy armour developed to protect the feudal horseman in the violence of close combat. The bow's penetrative power, even at short range, was far too slight. In the later tenth century the crossbow appeared in Europe, a kind of medieval equivalent of the anti-tank gun. It may have been a Western invention, or it may have been copied from Chinese types. Whatever its origin, it was developed and improved in the West until it became the most lethal infantry weapon of its time. Even when the English longbow began to assert its dominance of the European battlefields in the fourteenth century, the crossbow was preferred for certain tasks. The crossbow was used for another century until both weapons were superseded by firearms.

The equivalent to the crossbow, in the field of artillery, was the *trebuchet* (catapult). In the early twelfth century, it became the first machine to make use of the principle of gravity-drive; it marked a vast improvement in the torsion-driven catapults used in Roman times. Improvement there undoubtedly was, but by modern standards practical advance was slow. The creative medieval engineer and soldier were battling all the time with new principles and concepts, and not simply with the development and adaptation of existing ones. Yet within a century of the *trebuchet*, European thinkers were actively exploring the properties of explosive compounds and their application to warfare. We have already described Greek fire, a type of Byzantine flamethrower; primitive rockets and firework effects were known to the Chinese and used in other Asian civilizations. But to Europeans goes the first claim of harnessing this power to the projection of missiles. The first pictorial illustration of such a missile-thrower dates from the early years of the fourteenth century.

The last major topic to be dealt with in this section on the materials of war is military architecture. The history of the walled town goes back to the very dawn of civilization. The walls of Biblical Jericho may have enclosed the earliest urban society in the world. The magnificent remains of Celtic earthworks in Britain remind us, too, of the long tradition of fortification developed by all settled communities up to modern times. The walled towns of Medieval Europe were in this long tradition, but in the castle her architects developed something that was virtually a new *genre*. The Roman *castrum* and the Byzantine fortress were little more than walled enclosures or fortified barracks. Neither artillery nor siege warfare was far enough developed to challenge improvements in design. But the European castle developed between the mid-eleventh and mid-fourteenth centuries as one of the most complex and specialized types of building in the history of architecture. Improved artillery power and the *trebuchet* improvements in military recruiting and discipline allowed commanders to mount longer and longer sieges; the need existed in some areas to defend positions with much reduced garrisons. All these factors made the designer exercise his ingenuity to the full. The value of a castle was too great for an invading army to ignore. As long as the castles and their garrisons remained untaken, the defenders could harass the invaders' lines of communication and, when they withdrew, emerge from their refuge and regain control of the country.

During the Middle Ages the nations of northern Europe were land powers with few interests overseas. Even in the Mediterranean, no effective Western navy developed until the Catalan fleets of Spain began to extend their power in the thirteenth century and the Italian city states turned from the purely mercantile use of sea power. The tactics of naval warfare only slowly evolved as a distinct branch of military science. For most of the medieval period battles at sea were, in effect, infantry fights staged on floating platforms; the ships were often lashed together to provide the "battlefield."

The Carolingian horseman was protected by a metal cap and a mail coat reaching to the thighs (37). His shield was circular, measuring between two and three feet in diameter (38). By the tenth century the mail coat (hauberk) was in general use in Europe, and at the time of the Norman Conquest of England in 1066 it was either knee length or full length and might have a divided skirt (39). The warriors depicted on the Bayeux Tapestry are wearing an im-proved type of *casque* (helmet). Its steeply conical shape deflected blows from above it; it is fitted with a nose-piece or "nasal." The long, kite-shaped shields protected the horse-man from shoulder to stirrup on his exposed and vulnerable left side (40). Mail shirts at earlier times had consisted of metal discs sewn on to a leather jerkin, but by the twelfth cen-tury ring mail with its greater flexibility was preferred. However, this was very costly as it

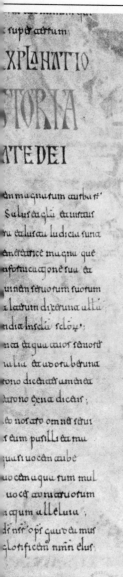

37

39

was made by laboriously sewing together individually forged metal rings. There might be as many as 100,000 rings to a suit (41, 42). For nearly four hundred years the mail coat was the chief form of armour. By the mid-thirteenth century it encased the whole body, and was provided with leggings, a hood and mittens for the hands. Then in the 1280s, to cope with the developments in offensive weapons, armourers began to reinforce the mail with metal plates at vulnerable points. At this time the surcoat, adopted from the Crusaders who used it to protect themselves from the sun, became a general part of a knight's armour, and was used to display his heraldic blazon (43 and page 41). The helmet, too, was larger. It now rested on the shoulders to give extra protection and to take the weight of the blows from the neck.

40

41

42 43

Since the eighth century, the horse had been the distinguishing companion of the European knight. The heavier *destrier*, as it was called, was the ancestor of the modern shire horse; it had to be immensely strong to carry the heavily armoured knights (44). With infantry improvements in the fourteenth century, however, the horsemen found themselves in danger from bolts and arrows. Plate armour, which could deflect these missiles, had to be developed (45). It was common for the knights to leave their horses at the rear of the battle and to fight on foot themselves. The armourers learned how to make superb custom-built suits which fitted so well that the weight of metal was hardly felt by the wearer (46). The armourer had to be an expert metal-worker, and to understand every detail of the human anatomy. Some of his finest achievements were suits of foot armour designed for the joust;

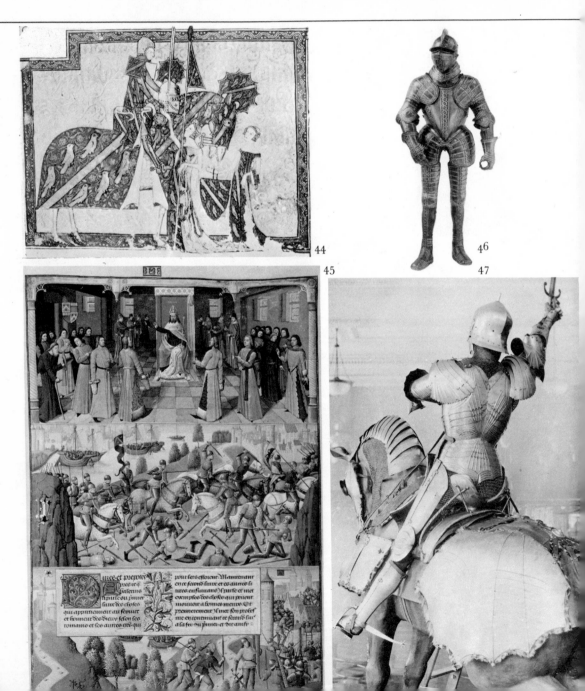

44

45

46

47

they have been called "masterpieces of hollow sculpture" (47, 48). Additional plates protected weak points such as the joints—knees, elbows and shoulders. Another great problem was to design a helmet that allowed the best visibility combined with maximum protection. Many variants were tried. For example, hinged visors with pointed snouts, and others of simpler design (49). Even the best of these helmets, with their lining and straps, made it more or less impossible to turn the head without having to turn the whole body; and the field of vision was still very restricted (50). The conflicting requirements of manœuvrability and massive protection posed the continuing and central dilemma of the medieval armourer.

48

49

50

28   The barbarian tribes that burst into Roman Europe were the ancestors of the medieval states; they took their names from their national weapons. The Franks were so called from the *francisca*, a throwing-axe; the Saxons took their name from the *scramasax*, a long, heavy, one-edged knife (51). The barbarians also used spears which developed into the Carolingian cavalry lance. The lance was fitted with a crosspiece behind the blade so that it did not penetrate too far into the body of the enemy (making it difficult to remove). Later a stout strip of linen was found sufficient, and this became the decorative pennon (52). The cavalry sword was a massive, two-edged, straight blade with a blunt point (53). This sword could cleave all but the stoutest armour. Helmets were designed to deflect direct blows, which could stun the wearer even if they did not actually pierce the metal. Knights also

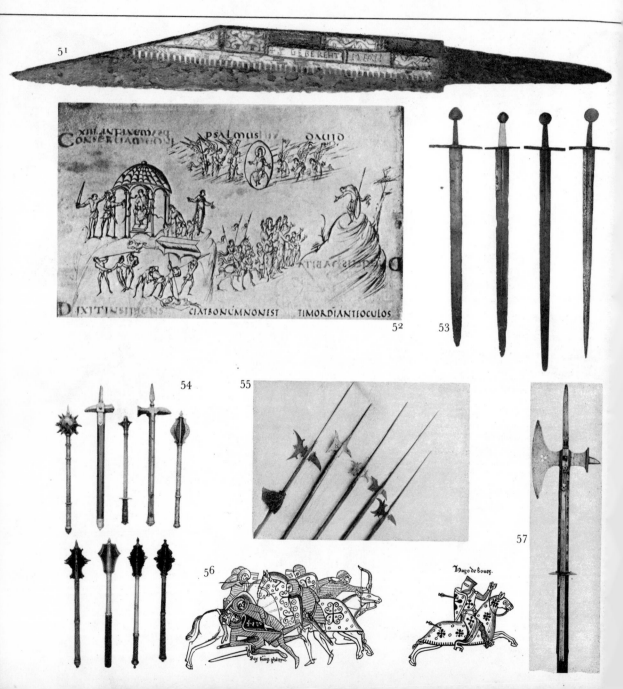

51

52   53

54   55

56   57

carried a mace and a ball-and-chain weapon with which to bludgeon their opponents. Maces were the preferred weapons of warrior bishops, common enough when great ecclesiastics were also feudal tenants, so that they would observe the letters of prohibition on shedding blood (54). In the fourteenth century the knight became vulnerable to new infantry weapons, such as the sixteen-foot Swiss pike, as well as the improved bows (55). Even the best horse armour could not prevent arrows maddening the animals with wounds in the flanks and legs (56). Even knights had to fight on foot. The shield was abandoned to leave both hands free to wield the still larger swords and a range of staff weapons such as the pole-axe which were introduced for the dismounted man-at-arms (57). Combats with such weapons became a standard feature of the tournament in the later Middle Ages (58).

58

30 The crossbow (59, 60) was both powerful and destructive. It easily pierced armour and made a terrible wound. Indeed, in 1139 Pope Innocent II issued an ineffective bull forbidding its use on humanitarian grounds, with as much effect as the modern Geneva convention governing chemical and biological warfare. Consisting of a short bow mounted on a wooden stock, it was fired by a trigger and could be aimed from the shoulder like a hand gun.

Introduced in the late tenth century, it was made of laminated yew and whalebone and later of high-tensile steel. As the tension increased, methods of drawing the bow improved. A hook at the bowman's belt enabled him to pull back on the string with the full weight of his body. Later a lever, fitted into lugs on the stock, was used. Finally, about 1400, a cranked windlass—removable before firing—was fitted (62, 63, 64). This type, called the *arbalet*, was

more lethal than early hand guns. The crossbow was at its best in siege warfare (65), when, from behind castle battlements bowmen could inflict terrible fire. The besiegers, both bowmen and gunners, vulnerable while reloading, used *pavises* (heavy shields) to protect themselves (61). These were fixed in the ground or worn on the back. They were too expensive to form the standard equipment of national levy troops. But a professional force of crossbowmen were a valuable asset to any commander, and from the twelfth century companies of mercenaries found regular work. The disciplined band of Faulkes de Brauté did much to help the royal cause in the barons' wars of early thirteenth-century England. Most famous of all crossbowmen were the Genoese, used by many a Continental captain.

The crossbow was never widely used by English armies. From the late thirteenth century onward, they evolved their famous national weapon, the longbow (67). This improved on the shortbow (68) as much as the crossbow had done. While the crossbow increased the range and penetrating power of the old weapon through greater tension in the bowstave and mechanical aids to draw it, the longbow achieved the same results by increasing the length of the bowstave. In this way it increased the travel of the string during which it imparted its impetus to the arrow. Formerly the bow had been drawn back to the chest, now it was pulled back to the ear (69). Apparently invented in South Wales during the twelfth century it was adopted by the English during the Welsh and Scottish wars of Edward I. With it, English armies often with bodies of Welsh archers (70), won great victories in France (71).

67

68

69

No other army really used it. Technically the weapon was simple. It was a yew stave measuring between five and six feet, with a central diameter of an inch and a half, tapering to ends which terminated in notched horn tips (72). Between these was stretched the string which would be taken off and coiled up when the weapon was not in use. But the archer needed years of practice from boyhood to develop the skill and the strength to use it.

Archery became a traditional English sport (73). At the moment of release the archer's arms were in a state of tension, keeping the bow at full stretch, while it required a pull of about 100 pounds to draw the string—about twice the pull required in modern sporting bows. The range was about 200 yards and the heavy "sheaf" arrows could pierce armour at half this distance. For the longer range the lighter "flight" arrow was used.

The Roman catapult and medieval mangonel (74) had consisted basically of a wooden beam, hollowed at one end to receive the missile, and tensed at the other between twisted ropes. The beam was forced down horizontally, and then released upward. The projectile, weighing up to 60 pounds, was catapulted forwards in a low trajectory, to a range of about 400 yards. In the twelfth century Europe acquired a new weapon—a wooden beam pivoted on a vertical frame and set in motion by men pulling on ropes (75). Cumbrous manpower was soon replaced by a massive counterweight, which dragged the beam down, before it was released: this was the high-trajectory *trebuchet*. Its range was no more than 300 yards (76), but in siege operations its calibre counted for more than its range. The next major advance was the use of gunpowder (77). The first cannon fired arrows, but cannon-balls were soon in com-

74

75

76

77

mon use (78). The gunpowder was often too powerful for the guns and the firing-tubes often burst. The first European mention of a salt-petre powder was made in the 1260s by Roger Bacon (79), in his *De secretis operibus*. Cannons were used by the English at Crécy in 1346, but to little effect. In these early days the powder did not ignite quickly, and the gun had to be packed with rags and waste, to build up pressure for powerful explosion. Later the powder was improved. During the fifteenth century, the huge bore of the early guns was reduced to give a higher muzzle velocity (pages 42 and 43). The gun could also be used as an anti-personnel weapon (80). The first small-bore guns consisted of a number of small tubes fixed to a carriage, which could be fired rapidly by dragging a match across the touch-holes. Hand guns only became effective in the fifteenth century (81).

78

79

80   81

36   The first castles were no more than wooden towers. Duke William of Normandy brought a prefabricated wooden tower to England in his invasion fleet in 1066 and assembled it when he landed (82). In the ninth century English castles were built as refuges from Viking and Saracen invaders. Emperor Charles the Bald ordered the building of castles in Germany in 862. Wherever possible stone was used for these simple towers, from an early date. The tower consisted of a ground-floor storage room with a well at its centre. Above was a hall to accommodate the lord and his followers. In time, the tower incorporated more rooms and grew in size. The central keep of the Tower of London, built by William the Conqueror, is the finest surviving example of the basic tower castle (83). A popular defensive device was to have the main entrance at first-floor level. This could only be approached by a wooden stair

82

83 84

that was thrown down if the building came under attack. Castles developed late in England, but after the Norman Conquest hundreds were put up all over the country, of the motte-and-bailey type (84). At its simplest this was a tower on a hillock (the motte) surrounded by an enclosure (the bailey) with storage buildings protected by a palisade and a moat. Celtic earthworks sometimes provided a ready made bailey (85). During the twelfth century, as siege techniques improved, square towers were replaced by round ones, in order to be free of vulnerable projecting corners (86). The round shell keep, such as the one at Restormel in Cornwall, was a transitional type (87). In Italy, where aristocrats tended to live in the towns, their towers dominated the scene (88).

85 86

87

88

In the twelfth century, castle design culminated in the magnificent Chateau Gaillard built in Normandy by King Richard I (1157–99) of England. The site, all-important to the castle builder, is superb, its cliffs falling steeply away on three sides. The great keep is protected behind an inner bailey and a middle bailey (89). Gaillard is a "concentric" castle, its keep surrounded by two or three outer walls. The finest concentric castle is the Crusader castle of Krak des Chevaliers in modern Syria (90). Complicated arrangements of towers, protected gates and ramps, forced the attacker who once breached the walls to follow a route chosen by the defenders. Both these forbidding fortresses, provisioned for a year, fell only by treachery. Garrison morale was crucial. Castles such as Castle Coca were vital in holding the lands reconquered from the Arabs. On the eastern frontier of Christendom the Teutonic

89

91

90

Knights built castles in Lithuania (91). The finest example of a medieval town is Carcassonne in southern France (92). The town walls defended these rising trading centres from hostile armies, local brigands and rapacious noblemen. Even churches sometimes doubled as castles in time of need. The fortress, like the church of Albi in the south of France, was built after the semi-independent Provence had been savagely put down by northern armies with the Church's blessing (93). The English King Edward I (1239–1307) built a ring of massive fortresses around Snowdonia, all with water access, to ensure his conquest of the Welsh principality. Caernarvon was the base of his military government, and in its shadow a famous walled town was built (94). The castle of Beaumaris laid out on a flat site without natural advantages, was a belated but fine example of the "concentric" plan (95).

92 93
94 95

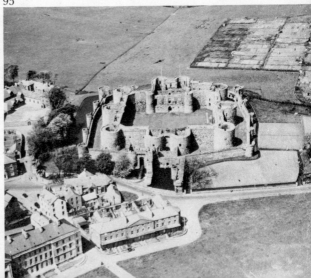

Medieval naval warfare was mainly coastal marauding, or "land battles" fought on floating platforms, provided by the enemy ships. In the North, the typical merchant ship was the short, wide-waisted cog (pages 44 and 45 *top*). In war, governments took them for transports or naval engagements (96). King Edward III (1327–77) repeated English land tactics by flanking each ship carrying men-at-arms with shiploads of archers (97). The archers cleared the enemy decks before the main attack. In the Mediterranean the calmer weather conditions and absence of tides made the fast, oared galley, later mounted with a bow gun, a valuable fighting ship (98). The kingdom of Aragon's power was based on its navy. The other Mediterranean powers were Islamic; the corsairs of the Barbary coast and later, the Turks (99).

98

96 97

99

Facing page A mounted knight from Tuscany wears his heraldic blazon on his surcoat (from page 25)

French miniaturist's view of a siege, with large-bore cannon and
small-bore hand guns (from page 35)

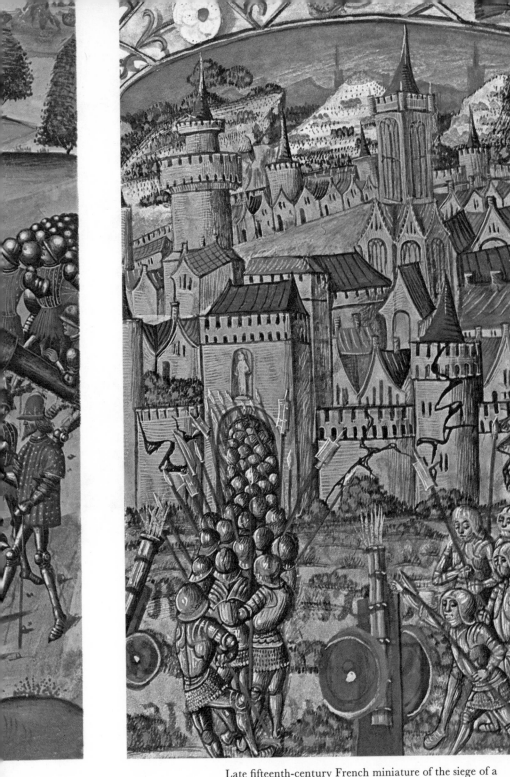

Late fifteenth-century French miniature of the siege of a walled town, showing typical early small-bore guns strapped together (from page 35)

43

A town under attack from the sea (from page 40)

Above Fleet of fifteenth-century French merchantmen being used as naval transports in time of war (from page 40)

Right These charging cavalrymen of fourteenth-century France use stirrups to meet the impact of a head-on collision (from page 60)

FRIDERIC' ROMAN'
·IMPE·   RATOR·

Left The great twelfth-century German Emperor, Frederick Barbarossa. _Above_ Mounted German knights and tents. The German Empire was a great military force in the Middle Ages (from page 66).

Overleaf: Top left Shields, helmets and surcoats were decorated with heraldic emblems (from page 74). _Bottom left_ French forces using cannon in the siege of a walled and moated town (from page 76). _Top right_ Wide-bore cannon held in readiness for a siege by King Henry of Navarre at Bordeaux (from page 76). _Bottom right_ Soldiers mining under the walls of a besieged castle (from page 77).

A prince is taken prisoner, from among his sleeping guards. The captors of important personages might win not only much prestige but also large ransoms. Noble prisoners were usually treated with courtesy by their noble enemies (from page 78).

Top English ships carrying armour-clad troops to Brittany. The ships carry the red cross of St. George and the banners of a royal prince (from page 83).
Left The much-feared Swiss halberdiers' weapons could cleave the toughest armour (from page 89).
Right Fierce hand-to-hand fighting between the English and French (from page 92)

La Mezquita: Islamic architecture at Cordoba, Spain (from page 105)

A medieval army of the fifteenth century on the march, with
mounted knights, infantry and baggage waggons

A battle episode in the Hundred Years' War

CHAPTER THREE
LORDS IN WAR AND PEACE

MEDIEVAL WARFARE is coloured by tales of chivalry and romantic legends of gallant Crusader knights charging down the enemies of Christ, and indeed there is much truth in this. The crack troops were the heavily armoured knights; the foot-soldiers were usually a rabble of reluctant peasants. England was the first country to recruit more reliable fighting men, including mercenaries. During the Hundred Years' War (1338–1453) between England and France, the profits from foreign war encouraged many a longbowman to become a mercenary. By then, however, the horseman's long supremacy in battle was doomed. The mounted soldier was more than a military machine; he was a symbol of landed privilege in European society. His armour and sword were costly, as were his horses. The battle order reflected the social system, loosely termed "feudalism." When a great man was granted land by the King, he became the King's liegeman and promised to answer his call to battle, armed and ready to serve. The land gave him the necessary income.

The huge privileges and tax exemptions of the medieval nobility were sometimes justified on the pretext that it was they who provided the nation with its fighting men. Perhaps it was an unconscious sense of their indefensible social privileges that made the French aristocracy so slow to yield to the realities of military science in the fourteenth century, and to charge to their deaths in a hailstorm of English arrows. Once the "fighting class" dismounted, their superiority to the peasant footmen was no longer symbolized. What were the origins of "feudalism"? In the 730s Charles Martel began to confiscate Frankish Church estates for the benefit of his lay nobles. At the same time, it seems the Franks began to fight on horseback.

Within a generation, the characteristic Frankish mode of war was for a line of heavy horsemen with lance at rest under the arm, to charge down their enemies and deliver a terrific blow from the lance. To equip and maintain one of these specialist warriors might cost as much as the plough teams needed for a dozen peasant families. But to be effective, this new technique needed a massed enemy and a formal set battle. Ironically, Europe's most serious external dangers during the next century were the elusive sea raiders from the North and South, and the fast-riding Magyar horsemen from Asia. The new cavalry ideas developing on the Continent were first applied in England on that fateful day in 1066 when Duke William of Normandy defeated King Harold's English army at the battle of Hastings. During the early and high Middle Ages, the mounted warrior was the lord of the battlefield as he was the lord of the countryside. But a battle like Tinchebrai (1106) in France which the English King Henry himself and other of his knights fought on foot, is a reminder that infantry power was by no means forgotten.

By the fifth century, the army of the Western Roman Empire had long been dominated by contingents from the barbarian tribes brought in as allies or *foederati* from beyond the frontiers (100). Their commanders, like Roman generals before them, struggled for control of the seats of power in the capital. In the winter of 406, waves of Germanic tribes crossed the Rhine and by the end of the century Europe had become the battleground of rival semi-barbarian states. The most far-flung people were the Vandals who crossed the European continent to Spain; they were then driven out from Spain by the Visigoths and settled in Africa. In this rich Roman province they established a society dominated by a horse-riding aristocracy (101). But they were defeated in the mid-sixth century by the armies of the Eastern Emperor Justinian (102). The Visigoths of Spain also rode to battle on horse-

102

back. But in the early 700s their state was overrun by the armies of Islam which advanced over the Pyrenees and were not defeated until 733 (by Charles Martel at the famous battle of Poitiers). This Arab defeat was due largely to the Arabs' own divisions inside Spain, but the threat accelerated military reforms introduced by Charles Martel. The army of the Merovingian kingdom (103), which Martel effectively ruled, had been largely an infantry force; the throwing-axe or *francisca* was its main weapon. The Merovingians were threatened not only by the Saracens from the south but also the Frisians in the north. By giving them a revolutionary new cavalry, Martel greatly strengthened them. Many acres of Church land were granted by charter to laymen to pay for this new force.

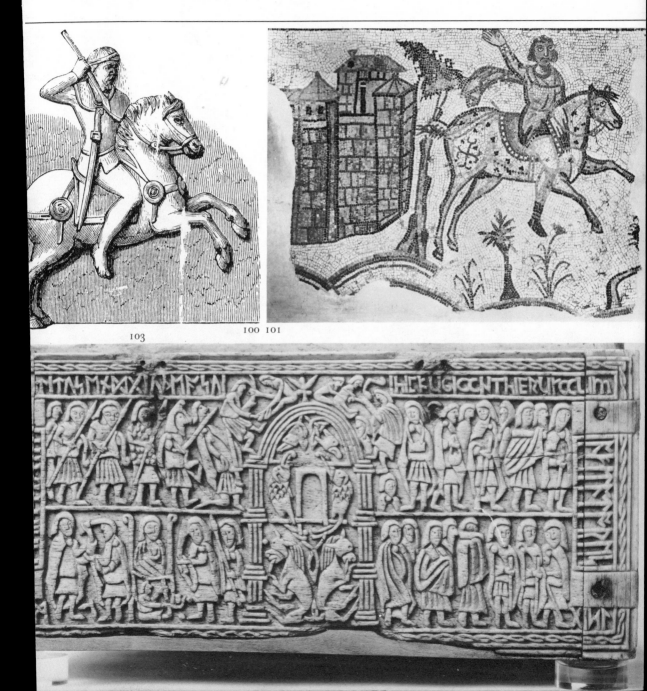

103

100 101

No one doubts that heavy feudal cavalry originated in the mid-eighth century, but the reasons for this have not been entirely clear. Modern research indicates that behind this military revolution lay a small but vital improvement in the use of the horse—the introduction of the stirrup (104). Combined with the high saddle, the stirrup gave the sword- or lance-bearing warrior a secure seat on his mount (105). For added security he could stand in the stirrups while exchanging blows with the enemy. It was the genius of Charles Martel, or one of his advisers, that saw how the stirrup could allow the horseman to charge an enemy with lowered lance and still hold his balance under the force of the impact (106 and page 45 *bottom*). From that time on the armoured man, his horse and his lance became a thundering human missile. No body of infantry then known could hope to resist a

104

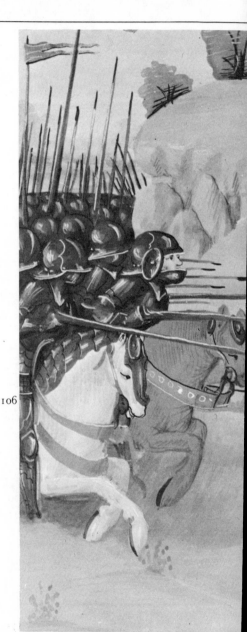

106

105

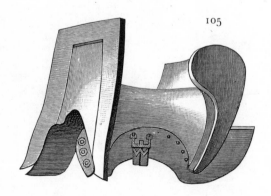

charge of such weight, and the old-style cavalryman would be unhorsed at the first encounter with this modern rider. It is thought that the stirrups we know originated in China; there are pictures of them in Chinese sources from the sixth and seventh centuries (107). The earliest known Western depiction dates from about the year 800. Yet all sorts of evidence proves that the object itself was known in the West at least seventy years earlier. We know from near-contemporary records that the Frankish army was a mounted force by the end of the eighth century and the infantry had been relegated to a subordinate role. About this time, the *francisca* and the barbed throwing-javelin were gradually dropped from the standard equipment. The *spatha*, the early short sword, was lengthened to become the heavy cavalry sword that only a man using stirrups could wield (108).

107

108

Equipped with his new army (109) the great Emperor Charlemagne (110) (died 814) was able to establish his authority throughout the Western European continent. He even defeated the warlike Lombard kingdom of northern Italy. Picture (111) shows the Lombard crown. But the limitations of his new force were revealed by the fact that it took the Emperor thirty years of campaigning to force the pagan Saxons to Christianity. In the marshy and forested area that was then Saxony, the Saxons were able to harass and defeat the imperial army by sudden raids. Yet eventually Charlemagne secured the northern frontier, just as he pushed Christian authority across the Pyrenees for a brief period. He was one of the great generals of all time and his achievements were considerable. In most years, he began his campaigns in May, when the grass was long enough to provide fodder for the horses on the

109

111

110

march; the campaigns ended in the autumn. He drew his soldiers from those parts of his empire near the theatre of operations. His tactics were to break up the enemy line by a charge, and then to destroy him piecemeal in a series of individual combats in which the heavier swords of the Carolingian cavalry would have the advantage. Some of the knights would be equipped with bows. All carried small round bucklers and wore cuirasses (chest armour) and steel caps (112). The chapel at Aachen symbolizes Charlemagne's grand imperial dreams. But soon after his death in 814 his sons were fighting over the inheritance, and the inhabitants of the newly formed "empire" were cowering in terror behind ruined Roman walls, seeking shelter from the attacks of Vikings, Saracens and Magyars (113).

112
113

The military and technical bases of the feudal system have been described. Many other factors were important, too. For example, threats from outside raiders during the ninth century led many small men to seek the protection of their more powerful neighbours (114). In Italy and southern Europe the danger was from the Saracens or Arabs (115). Apart from the main conquest of Spain, many independent Islamic chieftains terrorized the coasts and even penetrated inland. One chieftain was able to establish himself for a while in the foothills of the Alps, and to prey upon the traffic there. In the North were the terrible Vikings. In their Scandinavian homelands the Viking people were developing a considerable culture; archaeology has revealed examples of their expert metal-working (116). But to the settled communities of England, Ireland and France they seemed

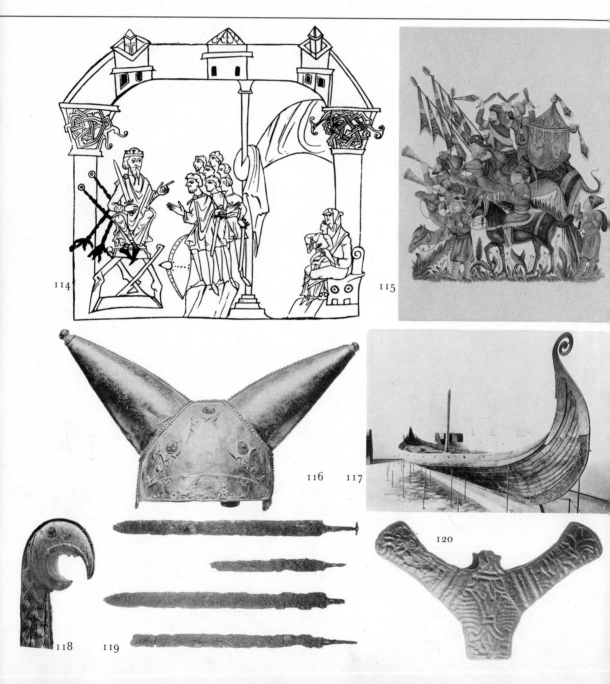

114

115

116   117

118   119

120

fierce and destructive barbarians. Their superbly built longships with their carved prows struck fear into the peasant population as they navigated up the rivers (117). Behind the painted shields, hung over their sides, sat the warrior-oarsmen. As soon as the boat made landfall they leapt out and scoured the vicinity for horses with which to make lightning raids inland. Their weapons were the axe and the sword; their round shield and helmets were often decorated with horns and other emblems (118, 119, 120). The Vikings left burning villages behind them; many peasants were killed, others were taken to be sold into slavery. The Northmen even tried to besiege Paris (885–7) but this was not their natural type of warfare and they were driven back (121).

121

At the battle of Lechfeld in 955 the German Emperor Otto I defeated Magyar armies who for a hundred years had menaced the eastern frontiers of the German Empire. After Lechfeld they ceased their depredations, and by A.D. 1000 had become a Christian kingdom. The German Empire grew to be the greatest power and force in Europe (page 47). As the Middle Ages advanced, German armourers won a European reputation for their skill (122).

One of the greatest twelfth-century Germans was Emperor Frederick Barbarossa who aimed to assert German supremacy in northern Italy (page 46). But at the fateful battle of Legnano, 1176, his German cavalry was defeated by the Lombard infantry militia (123). The Norman Conquest of England in 1066 ranks as a major turning-point in the history of warfare. At the battle of Hastings mounted shock combat, long known on the Continent,

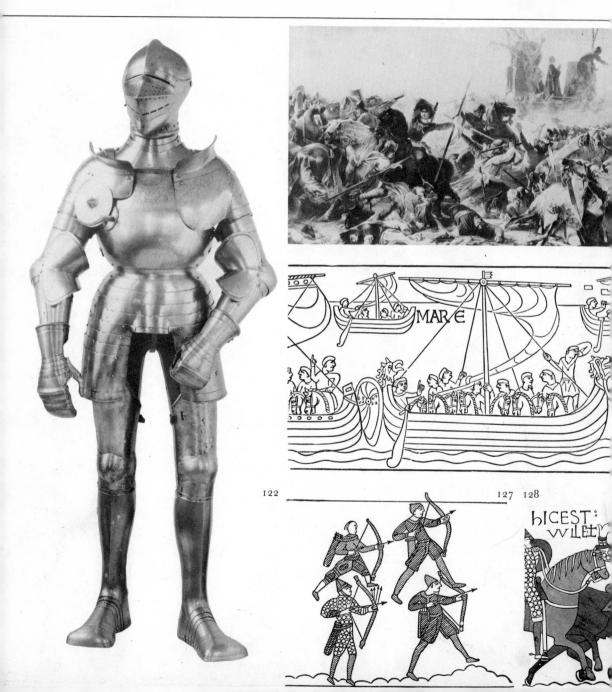

122

127 128

hICEST: VVLEt

finally came to England. Yet William the Conqueror had luck, too. To assemble a fleet large enough to carry his troops across the English Channel was not easy, and for weeks the winds blew against him (124). But William eventually landed unopposed at Pevensey Bay on the south coast. Harold learned the news on 1st October (125) and hurried south from Stamford Bridge. The English dismounted to form the traditional shield wall (126). William had not only a trained cavalry but a body of archers (127). At one point, Duke William raised his helmet to prove he still lived (128). Late in the day, thinking their enemies beaten, the English broke ranks. Disorganized, the axemen had no hope against the Norman Cavalry. His army scattered, Harold fought on, but was himself killed (129) only days after his last victory over the Norwegian army at Stamford Bridge had seemed to guarantee his crown.

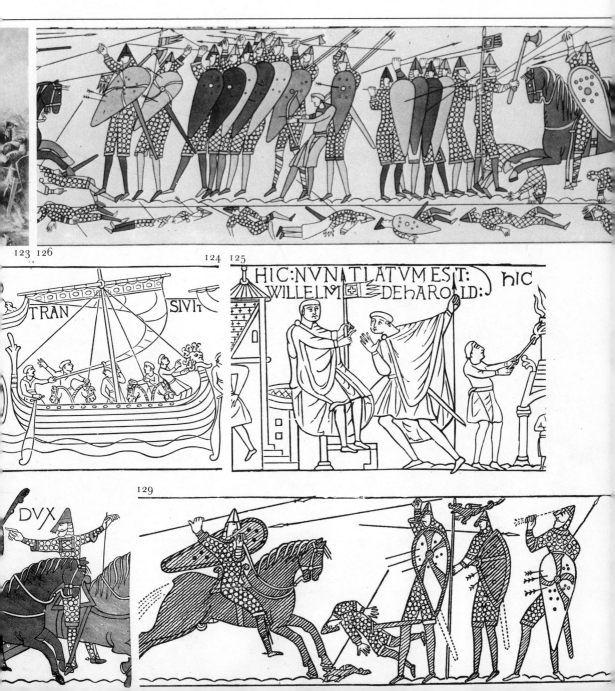

123 126

124 125

TRAN SIVIT

HIC:NVNATLATVM EST:
WILLELM DEHAROLD: hIC

129

DVX

68   During the thirteenth century the trade routes of Asia, from China to Persia and thence to Constantinople, lay at peace under the Mongol emperors (130). Few military leaders have a blacker reputation than Genghis Khan (1162–1227), the first of the line (131). Atrocity was systematically used; with primitive logic he showed some clemency to those who capitulated—those who resisted he killed or drove from their cities (132). But the army that won his victories was a disciplined well-led force. After the battle everything was permitted, but death was promised to any warrior who turned to plunder before victory was assured. A hardy nomadic race, the Mongols were the ideal material for a conquering army. Used to living off the land, and horsemen from birth, Mongol warriors moved free of cumbersome baggage-trains and at lightning speed (133). But their supremacy in battle was due to careful general-

130

131
132

133

ship. Their plan of battle was conventional enough. The army was deployed with a centre of three lines—vanguard, main force, a rearguard—and wings. The tactical emphasis was upon surprise where possible, surrounding the enemy, and pursuing them to the death (134, 135). The chain of command reflected the social hierarchy—family headmen, tribal chiefs and district rulers holding successively higher commands. But the commander-in-chief was appointed on merit alone: two of Genghis Khan's finest generals were only in their twenties. Mounted bowmen were the crack troops of a Mongol army (136). In Europe at that time, the bow was still the weapon of the despised infantry but Mongol princes like the Khan Batu were proud to bear it.

134
135

136

Tamerlane (*c.* 1336–1405), who claimed to be the descendant of Genghis Khan, established his power at Samarkand, the capital of the Mongol Khanate of Turkestan. He conquered Persia and Mesopotamia and sacked Delhi, Baghdad, Aleppo and many other cities (137, 138). He broke the power of the "Golden Horde" Tartars in Russia, and the Ottoman Sultanate in Turkey, receiving the Sultan as a suppliant (139). He, too, used brutality as a means of policy but he was also a great general and his army was a tightly and well-organized force (140). Tamerlane studied his enemies' methods of battle and insisted upon good scouting while on campaign. Bravery he believed to be nothing more than patience in a tight spot; rashness was "the devil's daughter." Tamerlane laid down meticulously detailed standing orders for his commanders and if the enemy was more than 40,000 strong, he him-

137

138

self took command. The army's centre and wings were composed of three divisions which were designed to deliver nine separate blows against the enemy's position. The general's job was to direct the action, and only as a last resort was he to endanger his own life on the battlefield. The armament of Tamerlane's predominantly Turkish army was much as it had been in the days of Genghis Khan. In those days the soldiers' chief reward had been plunder, but under Tamerlane there were fixed scales of military pay. Compared with European practice of the time this Asian army and its battle plan was positively scientific. Tamerlane insisted upon absolute obedience. The results show how well this paid off, for he had a career of conquest such as the world has rarely seen.

139

140

CHAPTER FOUR

SOLDIERS AND CHEVALIERS

THE FEUDAL SOCIAL SYSTEM, which linked land tenure with military duty, made the specialist type of mounted combat the hallmark of the upper rank of society. At first, only the rich landowner could afford the expensive horses and equipment; his lavish mode of battle reinforced his superiority in the social sphere. The war-horse became the symbol of a social stratum as well as of a military technique. The mounted warrior who found himself disinherited, or for any other reason lacking the lands needed to maintain his social station, sometimes became literally a "free lance" or wandering knight. Such men were often the younger sons of great houses who could expect only a small inheritance from their father. They thronged the courts of Europe as hangers-on. For them war could mean the chance of a fortune, or at least rich presents from the ruler for whom they fought. If they had the good luck to capture a wealthy prisoner, his ransom money might buy them the hand of a rich heiress and allow them to enter the ranks of the landed aristocracy.

Since warfare could enrich the landless warrior, it was vital to him that there should be regular conflicts. During the eleventh century, it was apparently thought that the supply of suitable wars was drying up for, in the 1060s, an institution arose which can best be described as a friendly "mini war." In these early years the tournament, for such it was, could involve scores of combatants. They grouped themselves in two miniature opposing armies, and fought simply for the love of it. Weapons, tactics and everything else was done in earnest; men were wounded and even killed. More important to the less affluent combatants was the fact that any prisoners, taken according to the rules of the tournament, had to buy their freedom by paying ransoms. These might be simply the horse and weapons they were wearing when taken (rich prizes in themselves); but they could be far more valuable. One of the most famous medieval knights, William Marshal, became a rich man through his prowess in the tournament. He ended his life as Marshal of England and thanks to the rich heiress that his prestige enabled him to marry, lord of one of the greatest landed estates in the realm. William Marshal's name was a byword for knightly prowess and honour, but there were others whose mercenary intentions were not graced in this way. More and more this rough and costly "sport" was deplored by men of substance, many of whom were unwilling to risk their family inheritance to the lottery of a boisterous *mêlée*. Europe's rulers did everything possible to end a practice that provided the ideal meeting-place for large bodies of armed—and possibly discontented—vassals.

Side by side with this evolution, another strand was being woven into the fabric of European social life. In the twelfth century, partly inspired by the stirring example of the Crusaders, the rough and often brutal military class became filled with Christian ideals of community service and respect for the aged and weak. The men of war began to develop a sense of honour that owed much to the faith of the Christian Church. But this chivalry was unmistakably a layman's ethic, and it rapidly developed its own literature and conventions. The central hero of chivalric literature was the semi-legendary King Arthur; "histories" and epics of his life were produced from England to Germany, and his effigy carved into the portals of churches and cathedrals in Italy and France. The age of chivalry was the offspring of the military classes and is an essential part of the story of medieval warfare. But as the thirteenth century advanced, what had derived from the military pursuit began to feed back into it in some measure. Young men began to look upon war itself as an extension of the joust. There are many cases of battles being lost by rash and ill-disciplined horsemen launching a charge before the right moment, or by riding down their own infantry in their eagerness to engage the enemy. A fifteenth-century French chronicler referred to the siege of Neuss in 1476 as "a veritable school of honour," where young gentlemen might hope to learn much of the lore of chivalry.

While all this pageantry was developing around the business of mounted combat, the latter was already feeling the competition of new and lethal types of infantry developed in Switzerland and England. It is interesting that Edward III, who showed the Continent that the horseman's battle supremacy was doomed by the bowman, founded that first order of chivalry. It was some compensation, perhaps, to English knights who no longer rode glamorously to battle.

Of course, the glamour had never been more than skin deep. Battles were bloody affairs, and a long war could devastate a whole region, destroying crops and ruining rich and powerful cities. Since the twelfth century, European rulers had devised ever more effective ways of bringing soldiers to the battlefield as the obligations of feudal land tenure weakened. More and more European armies had professionals in their ranks; more and more men fought for pay or booty as part of a calculated financial venture. New "laws of war" sought to regulate matters relating to ransoms, the surrender of towns and the capture of prisoners-of-war. But these affected only the combatants. The code of knightly conduct that ordained mercy to the weak and defenceless was, in times of war, forgotten, and the civilian population in a battle zone fell victim to the age-old brutalities of war.

Yet during our period men attempted to find objective legal criteria that could be used to decide whether a war was a "just war." This was important not only because independent princes aimed to assert their exclusive right to levy war; but also because booty taken in an "unjust" war might have to be returned. In a society where disorder and conflict were rampant the border-line between war and rapine was shady. But it came to be accepted that sovereign princes indeed could levy war, if they did so to make good just claims, and that others could not. During the Middle Ages men often assumed that resort to war was a resort to God's judgement on a dispute. It was a lofty unrealistic notion perhaps, but not so much more absurd than some of our ideas today.

The nobility of Europe virtually lived in the saddle, whether hunting or fighting. Tournaments began as bloody and dangerous *mêlées*, and gave additional excuses for fighting. Early in the twelfth century the legend of King Arthur and his knights began to fire the European imagination (141). Later a young man wrote a book on the correct way of holding jousts on the Arthurian model, and even the dour soldier King Edward I (1272–1307) of England was a keen Arthurian, holding tournaments based on themes from the legend. The young bloods adopted the fictional arms of "Sir Kay" or "Sir Launcelot" for their combats in the lists. Serious heraldry was in fact a vitally important aspect of warfare. As armour came to conceal the horseman's body and face completely, some other identification was needed. Emblems on the shield, helmet and surcoat were quickly adopted. These

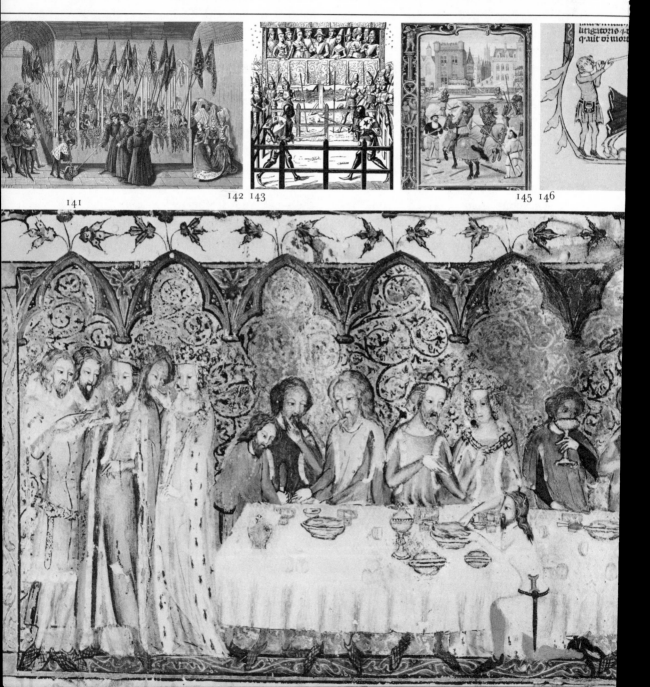

141

142 143

145 146

colourful blazons and crests were a central feature of the pageantry (142 and page 48 *top*). By the fifteenth century the joust was well organized. There were separate rules for combats on foot and on horseback (143). Opposing horsemen were usually separated by a wooden barrier to stop them colliding (144). The lists were policed by marshals who used long batons to separate combatants (145). Jousting lances were specially tipped to avoid fatal accidents (146). The tournament was the favourite sport of young noblemen. As the horseman lost his pre-eminence in battle, the long hours of practice at the quintain (tilting post) developed skills that were useful only in the mock battle of the lists (147).

144

147

The siege of a major town or fortress could last for months. The besieging army's camp with its princely pavilions and merchants' stalls was a bustling township in itself (148). The foundations of walls and towers were undermined by the besiegers. The mines (tunnels) and castle walls were shored up with timber which was set ablaze, bringing down yards of masonry and even whole walls. Even after cannons had appeared the mine was for a long time the best siege weapon (pages 48 *bottom* and 49 *top*). When speed was vital, shielded sappers (engineers) worked at ground level, pulling out the lower courses of masonry (page 49 *bottom*). *Trebuchets* were used to attack the walls, and siege towers were wheeled across filled moats to challenge the tops of the walls (149). If a castle was really secure, the attackers might set up walls and trenches of circumvallation (encirclement) to ensure

148 149
150 151

the garrison's starvation or demoralization. A besieged commander had to hold out as long as possible. The prelude to a siege came when a herald demanded the town's capitulation (150). If this was refused the siege was begun by artillery fire against the walls (151). Without artillery fire, there was technically no siege and the commander could surrender without staining his honour. This would spare the garrison and probably the lives of the townsfolk (152). If the place was taken by assault the conventions of war allowed the ruthless looting of all property and the slaughter of all soldiers and inhabitants for defying the besieging prince. In theory all booty was the property of the prince and it was gathered together for distribution. The capture of strategic towns was a major activity of later medieval war and a coastal fortress or seaport would be attacked from the sea (153).

152
153

The laws of war, or law of arms, governed many other things than the besieging of towns. In medieval war, the cause of hostilities was expressed as a personal quarrel between two princes or rulers. As a result, concepts of knightly honour—the code of the rulers of Europe—were very much to the fore. In a siege, for example, a prince who had once demanded the surrender of a town disgraced himself if he retired without taking it (154). In other matters of war, disputes were often settled in specially convened "courts of chivalry" composed of high-ranking knights (155). Even princes could be arraigned before such courts. The subject that most engaged the medieval soldier and caused most disputes, was the taking of prisoners (156 and pages 50–51). In the heat of battle, it was hard

154 1
158 1

to ensure that one's claim to a **prisoner** would be upheld, or that he would not surrender to someone else (158). When King John of France was taken at the battle of Poitiers he was in some danger of his life from the jostling of his rival captors. A lawsuit followed between the two chief claimants. The taking of ransom was lucrative to soldiers of all ranks (157). Clear rules on the subject were in everybody's interests. There was a recognized international system of conventional laws governing the proceedings of war. Heralds had the task of carrying messages relating to disputes between rival camps. The heralds were important functionaries and as such enjoyed immunity and the neutrality of an international fraternity. Even mercenary troops observed the privileges of heralds and the customs of war.

157

As the Middle Ages advanced, the old obligation to do military service in return for land often lapsed. The quality of troops raised in this way steadily deteriorated. In Italy, men in trade and industry were unwilling to lose manpower to the citizen's army. The *carrocia* (cart) that had once carried the Italian city emblem into battle was no longer the focus of a patriotic militia (159). In the fourteenth century, cities began to hire professional captains on a *condotta* (contract). The Englishman, Sir John Hawkwood (Giovanni Acuto), who served as a mercenary in Italy, recruited his troops from men seeking work in the lulls of the Hundred Years' War (160). There were German, Provençal and Italian *condottierri*. The latter were recruited from the poorer parts of Italy. The fifteenth-century Italian commanders led sizeable armies and often conducted policies independent of their em-

ployers. Sometimes they were executed for treason, sometimes they won glittering prizes. Baldassare Cossa became a pope, Francesco Sforza became Duke of Milan (161). Established princes in need of funds would even hire out their own armies. The most famous of these was Federigo da Montefeltro, Duke of Urbino (162). The *condottieri* were sometimes accused of holding back their armies, rather than fighting their employers' battles in earnest.

Such accusations were seldom justified (164) but nevertheless Italy was spared the worst barbarities of war until the French invasion of the 1490s. Men like Bartolomeo Colleoni (163), immortalized in Verrocchio's famous equestrian statue in Venice, were great men in Italy, but their refined tactics were no proof against massive invasion from outside (164).

160 161

162 163

Many other mercenary bands operated in Europe besides those led by the Italian *condottierri*. Most terrible were the *écorcheurs*. These were the bands of unemployed professional soldiers who roamed the French countryside when lulls in the fighting threw them out of work. Out-of-work mercenaries were the scourge of Europe during times of intermittent war. The principle of pay had been introduced in England by the kings themselves, as a way of improving the quality and discipline of the feudal host. King Edward I really developed the system and laid the foundations of England's military successes during the fourteenth century (165). To demand his traditional right to free military aid from powerful subjects caused political trouble, especially when the war was in France. Instead, he contracted or indented to pay chosen vassals for bringing an agreed number of soldiers to the campaign.

165

166

167

(Later, dukes and earls and even Edward the Black Prince were drawing daily wages on their contracts.) The feudal levy was still called out, but now the cavalry were grouped under distinguished commanders (bannerets) who carried square banners, the "colours" of their "regiments"; the royal dukes, of course, bore their own variants of the royal arms (166 and page 52). Edward I's military skill was not only in organization. His talents in the field had been shown when he led his father's royalist forces against the rebel baron Simon de Montfort (167). In the campaign of 1265 he outmarched the rebels, and forced them into an impossible position in the bend of the river at Evesham in the west of England (168). There was no escape, and de Montfort's army was destroyed.

168

Within some twenty years (1277–95) Edward I of England completed the subjection of Wales. The southern part of this country had been dominated by Anglo-Norman lords, based at castles like Caerphilly and Chepstow, for nearly two centuries (169, 170). But the mountain retreats of Snowdonia in the North had given refuge to a succession of bold Welsh princes. A main base of Edward's operation against the Welsh was Chester (171). He owed his success to command of the sea, the massive castles that he built like a containing wall round Snowdonia, and the tactical combination of horsemen and the longbow. Conway Castle on the north Welsh coast could, like all the others, be approached from the sea (172). While the English fleet controlled the coast the great castles could never be long out of English hands. But more importantly, while English ships policed the Menai Straits—be-

169 170

171

tween Wales and Anglesey—the Welsh leader Prince Llewellyn (173) was deprived of grain from the island of Anglesey, his main source of food. Yet Welsh resistance might have lasted much longer had it not been for the death of Llewellyn, killed at the battle of Orewin Bridge in December, 1282. The two armies were divided by a stream. In crossing the bridge the English cavalry would have to face a determined force of Welsh spearmen who could attack the vulnerable cavalry while the main English army was still waiting to cross. However, a little ford upstream was unprotected. The English archers were able to cross here and drive back the Welsh spearmen while the English cavalry passed the river unmolested.

172
173

The Welsh may have lost their great leader Llewellyn. But in Scotland on the death of William Wallace, hunted down after his army's defeat at Falkirk in 1303, the Scottish leadership was taken up by Robert the Bruce (174). There was no good military reason for the repulse of the English. The combination of cavalry and longbow, evolved against the Welsh, was just as potent, when properly used, against the solid formations of the Scottish spearmen (175). At Stirling Bridge in Scotland, the English commander, the Earl of Warrenne, foolishly sent his cavalry across a narrow bridge before the archers had had time to deploy (179). This lost him the battle (176, 177). At Falkirk, the ageing King Edward I took charge when his enthusiastic knights had made a few initial and fruitless charges against the solid rows of Scottish spears. Edward called off the cavalry and let the bowmen shoot the

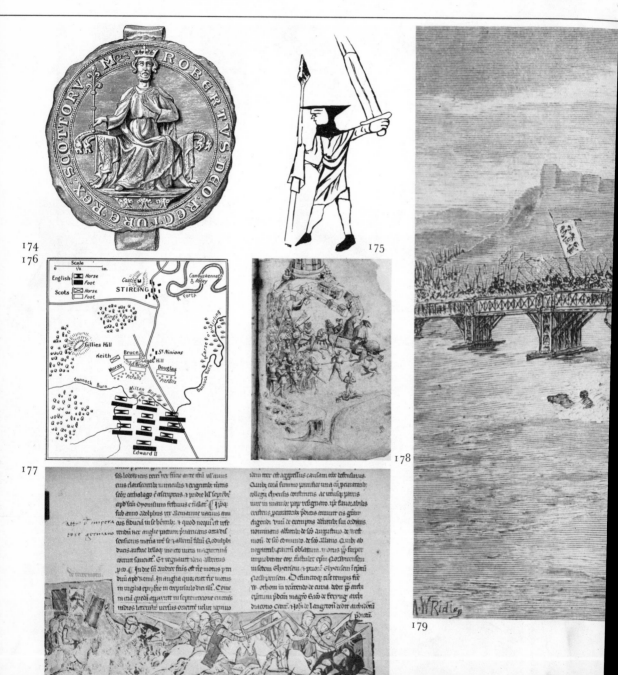

174
176

175

177

178

179

static Scottish formations to pieces, for the cavalry to finish off (178). Such an act had no chivalry in it, but it won battles. These Scottish campaigns taught the knighthood of England a lesson in war-making that would later win them laurels against the French. But first, there was to be humiliation to come. At Bannockburn in 1314 a small Scottish force routed the much larger army of Edward II of England. The English were forced to cross a treacherous bog before they could attack, and did so at night rather than use archers to cover a daylight crossing. The bold assault of King Robert the Bruce with his Scottish spearmen caught the English while they were still deploying and the small squadron of Scottish cavalry was sufficient to ride down the few English archers who did come into action.

88

English successes and failures in Scotland and Wales both pointed to the changes in European warfare. Battles were decided by how well the infantry, spearmen or archers, were used. Edward II's biographer compared Bannockburn with the great defeat of French chivalry at Courtrai (1302) by a citizen army of Flemings (180) who withstood the French charge and then drove the enemy horses remorselessly back into the little stream they had crossed

to attack. The secret was well-disciplined infantry. At Cassel (1329) (182) and Roosebecke (1382) the French horsemen could ride down less well-drilled Flemish levies. The Swiss developed an infantry of pikemen that could regularly defeat a mounted attack. The battle of Laupen in 1339 spelled out the end of the horsemen's superiority still more clearly. The battle was fought on an open plain, ideal for cavalry. Yet the Swiss, entirely un-

180

181 184

182

183 185

supported by cavalry, carried the day against Austria. The Swiss patriots evolved simple but effective tactics to deal with feudal invaders, even without a single commanding general. A Swiss army was a forest of pikes and the banners or standards of cantons, towns and districts (181, 183). Wearing light body armour, this infantry advanced at a rapid pace, the first four rows of pikemen holding their weapons at shoulder height with hands widely spaced and the point tipped slightly downwards. Around the standards were gathered the halberdiers whose heavy halberds—eight feet long handled axes—could cleave the toughest armour (184 and page 52 *left*). The Swiss gained a reputation that intimidated their opponents. The cantons hired out their troops as mercenaries, and to this day the gates of the Vatican are manned by Swiss guards (185).

Swiss infantry held the field in central Europe, until the Spaniards developed a superior tactic: their improvement in artillery made the massed phalanx suicidal. Meanwhile in the Hundred Years War between England and France, the longbowman was proving that the infantryman was superior in another way. This great conflict involved, or affected at one time or another, not only England and France but also the towns of Flanders, the kingdoms of Spain and parts of the German Empire (186). At the battle of Crécy (1346) King Edward III's English longbowmen won their first great Continental victory (187, 188). In a well-chosen defensive position, troops of men-at-arms were flanked by archers. The huge French army had come up with the small English force unexpectedly; King Philip of France ordered a halt, and planned to attack next day. But his order did not reach every unit and the

186 188

187 189

French army rolled forward into an ill-prepared attack. The Genoese crossbowmen on the French side hardly had time to discharge their first volley before they were driven down by the proud and impetuous French horsemen. Few of these even reached the English lines. Most were unhorsed or killed by the English arrows (189). Over 1,500 noblemen were killed in the French army, the English lost perhaps 150 men in all. Yet despite his massive victory, Edward III showed his strength as a general by forbidding the pursuit and holding his army intact (190). One of the commanders in the battle was the King's eldest son, Edward Prince of Wales, called the Black Prince. His armour now hangs in Canterbury Cathedral, a memorial to his reputation for chivalry and his brilliance as a military commander (191).

190 191

After Crécy, Edward III besieged and captured the port of Calais and so gained an important English bridgehead in France (192). But England was not strong enough to conquer Europe's greatest kingdom; English campaigns amounted to little more than raids (*chevauchés*). In 1355–56 Edward the Black Prince (193) led such a *chevauché* to Narbonne in the extreme South and then to Tours in the North. On returning to Bordeaux he was brought to bay by a large French army at Poitiers in September, 1356. He posted his men-at-arms and archers to the best advantage in the vineyards and hedges of a slight incline. The French led off with a cavalry charge that was easily repulsed by English arrows (194), but they followed up the charge with an attack by men-at-arms on foot. The English position was dangerous. Fierce hand-to-hand fighting ensued (page 53). The first French line drew

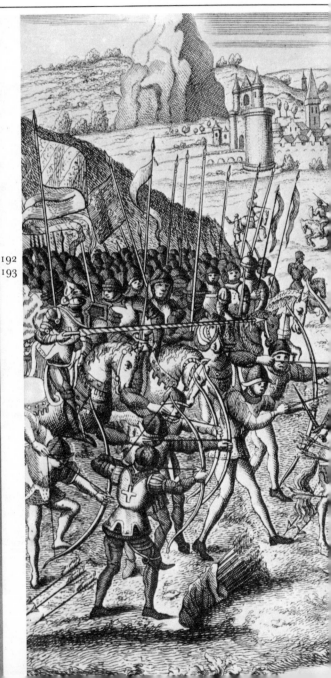

192
193

off and then, astonishingly the second line refused to advance. The third line led by King John (195) himself had nearly a mile to trudge in heavy armour before coming up with the English. Then with a brilliant tactical stroke Edward turned the scales by launching a cavalry charge. The French King was captured and the triumph of 1356 was even more complete than the victory of Crécy ten years before. The Black Prince's reputation for chivalry is belied by his brutal sack of Limoges. But such tactics could not win a kingdom. Realizing the superiority of the English in the field, the next French King—Charles V—avoided pitched battles and was content to harry the English and capture undefended towns. He was brilliantly assisted in this strategy by the practical generalship of Bertrand Du Guesclin (196).

194

195

196

Du Guesclin's unspectacular, semi-guerrilla tactics, had won back many of England's possessions in France. Henry V was determined to enforce the English claims to the French crown (197). His first campaign, with a small English army, began with the capture of Harfleur at the mouth of the River Seine, the first siege decided by the use of guns. Then he went on a *chevauché* through Normandy, pursued by a much larger French force. He had, however, ample time to prepare a fine defensive position flanked by the woods of Tramecourt and Agincourt. He drew up his small force of men-at-arms and archers, and when the French attack did not at first materialize Henry forced the issue by advancing his army (198). Now the French horsemen came on. Bogged down in the wet ploughland they offered easy targets, and the dismounted men-at-arms, crammed into congested space, could hardly move their

197

198

199

200

weapons. Many were knocked over by English archers wielding the heavy mallets used to drive in the sharp stakes that protected their lines. A false report that the French were attacking from the rear led the English to massacre their many rich prisoners. A fortune was lost in possible ransoms and the French nobility learned another bloody lesson. Henry V now attempted a systematic conquest of France, but died before he could succeed.

French morale was miraculously revived by the strange episode of Joan of Arc (199). Joan led the vital relief of the siege of Orleans in 1429 (200). Strategically the town was important, yet the French did not oust the English from their three-century rule in Bordeaux until 1453 (201, 202).

201

202

After English forces withdrew from France in the 1450s, there were many veterans needing employment. They found it in the civil wars at home, fought between the Yorkist and Lancastrian claimants for the throne. The leaders in these Wars of the Roses did not alienate public opinion more than absolutely necessary. An envious French chronicler noted that unlike the wars in France a generation earlier, the country at large was hardly affected. Towns were rarely attacked; artillery, the siege weapon *par excellence*, was little used. The commanders naturally adopted their usual tactics of longbow and men-at-arms, so neither side had a tactical advantage. But at the battle of Towton (1461) Edward of York ingeniously exploited the bowman's technique (207). A blizzard was beating into the faces of the Lancastrians and he ordered his archers to advance, fire a volley of heavy "sheaf"

arrows, and then retire. Assuming their enemies to be in easy range, the Lancastrians wasted their arrows with a heavy barrage directed against the wind. Edward always aimed to control London (208). In 1471, he landed in Yorkshire after a short enforced exile, evaded his enemies and reached the capital in a series of brilliant marches. Fog shrouded the ensuing battle of Barnet just outside London, and the Lancastrians, confusing the star emblem of the Earl of Oxford with the sun of York, fought their own reinforcements (209, 210). Fighting continued even when the mistake was known, for treachery was common enough. Indeed, in 1485 Richard III (211) lost the battle of Bosworth through treachery. At the last moment Lord Stanley changed sides, and the Earl of Northumberland in the rear failed to support the King.

208

210 211

207 209

Ce nom estet Albion
Il vous en plaist escouter

CHAPTER FIVE
WARRIORS OF GOD

WE HAVE NOW LOOKED AT military developments in the successor states to the Roman Empire from the late sixth century to the beginning of the modern period. We have seen how Byzantium continued the Roman tradition of scientific warfare, and evolved it into a sophisticated and adaptable system. In the West the invention (the word is hardly too strong) of shock cavalry tactics produced a revolution both in the conduct of war and in the organization of society itself. In the feudal order of things land was held in return for military service, and the flower of the army was the heavy mounted troops formed by the great landowners and their wealthier tenants and paid knights. The divisions of society were reflected on the battlefield. When in the fourteenth century that society began to change, as landed wealth was gradually threatened by the new commerce, so the forms of war changed, too. There is no suggestion of a simple cause-and-effect relationship here. One cannot say that because the power of towns grew in society at large so the infantry, the strength of the citizens' militia, came to dominate Europe's battlefields. But the parallels between social evolution and military developments were not entirely coincidental. The power of infantry first made itself felt after centuries of neglect, on the plains of Lombardy and in the battles of the Italian city states, in the victory of the towns of Flanders at Courtrai in 1302, in the successes of the

peasants and townsmen of the Swiss confederation and finally in the army of England.

Nowhere was the old socio-military organization of feudalism stronger than in France. The richest, and from the late twelfth century the strongest, nation in Europe, she witnessed the growth of an aristocracy that was wealthier, more independent and more exclusive in its privileges than that of England. Even the bitter defeats of Crécy and Poitiers could not destroy overnight the pride of the French chivalry, nor its conviction in its own superiority in war. Social status reinforced military conservatism. However, in the late 1300s, the French government began to adapt to the new military situation. France's catastrophic defeat by England at Agincourt (1415) was caused partly by a new generation of young bloods reverting to the practices of their forefathers. But by the end of the fifteenth century the French kings had brought a real professionalism into their army.

So far, however, we have omitted one central type of conflict, the religious war. Some of the finest military successes of French chivalry were won by expatriate Frenchmen in the lands of *outre-mer*—the successor states to the Crusades. The Crusades were in one sense a belated Western response to the lightning Islamic campaigns in the seventh century. Within a century the armies of Islam, fighting with the fury of religious conviction, had conquered Persia in the East and Spain in the West. They took in the Byzantine provinces in North Africa and Syria as well. The success of Islam was due in part to their fierce morale, in part to the weakness and disunity of the territories they overran, and in part to their military organization. We shall say something about this in what follows.

The Christian reconquest of Spain was a slow business. It began in the late eighth century and was not completed until 1492. In that year the last Moorish ruler was driven from his capital in Granada. For seven hundred years Christian and Muslim lived side by side on Spanish soil. During this time they learned much from one another. In terms of intellectual culture Europe was, by and large, the gainer, but in military affairs the Arab states copied much. In the twelfth century a form of Saracen heraldry arose as a result of contacts with Western knights both in Spain and in the Holy Land. Strong in the power of their new faith, the original Arab conquerors had carried all before them. But as they developed a settled civilization in their new territories the religious impulse weakened. For their part, the Christians lacked the resources to make a quick counter-attack and in any case became engrossed in their internal political rivalries. In Spain the central kingdom of Castile expanded as a land power, the state of Catalonia-Aragon on the east coast built up a Mediterranean empire. It took first the Balearic Islands and then exploited its naval power further to the east until Catalonians at last established themselves in Sicily and southern Italy.

Religious conviction can soon weaken as a driving force of conquest. But during the first burning years, fanatical enthusiasm is often enough to carry the day. But it is not always so. If the enthusiasts find themselves outclassed militarily they must either succumb, as did the Albigensian zealots of southern France in the thirteenth century, or they must evolve a new style of warfare. This the Hussites of Bohemia did. A religious minority within the German Empire, loyal to the teachings of Jan Hus who had been burned as a heretic by the Church in 1415, the Hussites suffered one attack after another from the knighthood of Catholic Europe. Yet thanks to deep inspiration, fine generals and a defensive tactic that fully utilized the new field artillery, the Hussites maintained their position throughout the middle years of the fifteenth century. The first major defeat of a Hussite force was inflicted by another when the movement split into rival factions.

The last of the "Warriors of God" were the Ottoman Turks. From small beginnings in the Anatolian provinces of Byzantium the Ottomans grew until they finally engulfed Constantinople itself. Their original impulse came from their conversion to the faith of Islam of which they became fanatical champions. Their empire, which had sprung from the conditions of a nomadic people in the Asian steppe, never lost the traces of its origin. It had to remain expansionist to live. In the sixteenth century Ottoman armies reached northward to the gates of Vienna and then as late as 1672 came a second siege. The crack troops of this formidable Ottoman war machine were the Janissaries, a body of slave soldiers recruited from the non-Muslim subjects of the Empire, and trained into a fanatical belief in Islam from boyhood. The Turks had begun their conquests centuries before as the true Warriors of Allah; the Janissaries were the natural heirs of the original religious impulse. In their case it was reborn with each new generation of converts.

The map of Arab conquests during the seventh century must make the spectator pause in astonishment. Syria and Egypt, Upper Mesopotamia and Persia all fell within decades, and the advance continued relentlessly onwards along the North African coast. In the 670s Arab ships were blockading Constantinople (212). The causes of this great military success must be sought, to some degree, in the political events outside Islam. In the 620s, by incessant campaigning the Byzantine Emperor Heraclius had broken the power of Persia, but in doing so he had also fatally weakened the strength of his own state. The Christian populations of the area were rife with heresy and discontent with the oppressive centralism of Constantinople. They welcomed the Arabs who allowed them to worship, in payment of a fine, undisturbed. But there was a more important cause. The troops of Islam were

21.

drawn at first from the warlike tribes of Arabia, but it was the genius of Mahomet that welded them into a united force. Islam was a religion of conquest and the mosque became the symbol of its success. Byzantine writers noted the Arabs' devotion to their fine swift horses and advised the use of archery aimed at the horses to disconcert an attack (213). The Arabs attacked in a single long deep line and came on confident of victory in the power of God. Later they adopted chain-mail tunics after the Western fashion (214) and their characteristic weapons were the curving sword (215) and the small round shield (216); they wore steel caps to protect their heads (217). Like most armies of the Middle East the Arabs also used horse archers (218).

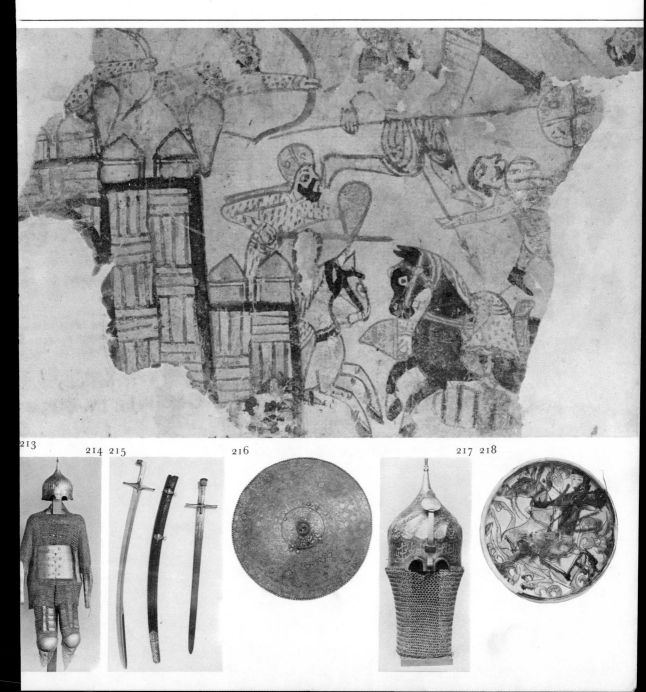

213   214 215   216   217 218

The Arab advance really exploded (632–44) under the first caliphs (Arabic word for the successors of Mahomet), Abu Bakr and Omar. Omar declared the *jihad* (holy war) that was to conquer the world for Islam. Coupled to the original religious impulse there had been an expanding pressure of population in Arabia. This, and the promise of paradise to all who died fighting the Infidel, intensified the religious drive and the crescent-topped banners were carried to China, India and the Pyrenees. As they spread further afield the Arabs came to adopt the culture and the military tactics of conquered peoples. Byzantium provided an important military model, though the mail-coated Arab lancers were faster than their opponents. Their raids on the Byzantine heartlands of Anatolia were gradually contained. In Spain they encountered the emergent Western heraldry,

219
220
221
222

which was adapted by Arab nobles to personal emblems on their shields and banners (219). The original conquerors had been housed in encampments, sometimes specially built, sometimes taken over from the conquered. Later they built their own great fortresses such as those in Spain (220) and the castle at Aleppo (221). The history of Islamic Spain is specially instructive as to the decline of the original impetus. Based on Cordoba (page 54) the first invaders built up a brilliant culture, but were gradually pushed southwards by the Christians. In the eleventh century a North African Berber dynasty displaced them and was in turn displaced by the Berber Almohade people in the twelfth century. Meanwhile Berber or Barbary corsairs were terrorizing the Mediterranean and Christian expeditions, setting out with great pageantry, had little success against them (222).

The First Crusade must be classed as one of the great military achievements in European history. A motley army drawn from northern and southern France, Lorraine and southern Italy, made its way to the distant land of Palestine (223, 224) forcing its way against an unfamiliar enemy to capture Jerusalem in 1098 (225). The senior lay leader was Raymond, Count of Toulouse, and the overall leader was Bishop Adhemar of Le Puy. The Bishop had been appointed by Pope Urban II who preached the Crusade at Clermont in 1095 (226). The Crusaders were greatly helped in their passage of the Balkans and in Anatolia, overrun by Turks, by the Byzantine Emperor Alexius I (1081–1118). The Crusaders' motives were a mixture of land hunger and religious enthusiasm. Zealous Western Catholics, they were suspicious of the Eastern Orthodox Church and admired their Turkish enemies

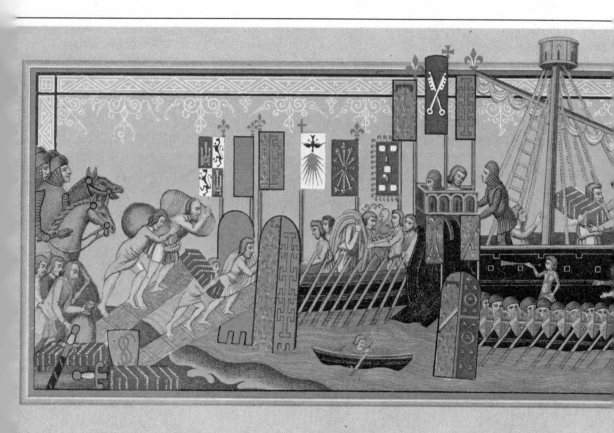

223

224 225

more than their Christian allies. The first great victory was over the Turks at the battle of Dorylaeum in June, 1097, in northern Anatolia. The Crusaders were marching in two widely separated armies when the first, Normans under Bohemond of Taranto, was attacked by the Turks (227). Against the light Turkish horse archers the weighty Frankish cavalry could do little. Throughout the morning the northern French held their ranks and suffered the rain of arrows. Then at midday their friends came up. They could now take the offensive, and when Bishop Adhemar appeared with a large force on the hills behind the Turks the enemy fled. Courage, discipline and intelligent generalship had won a great victory. The roads of Anatolia were open and the army moved on to the siege of Antioch.

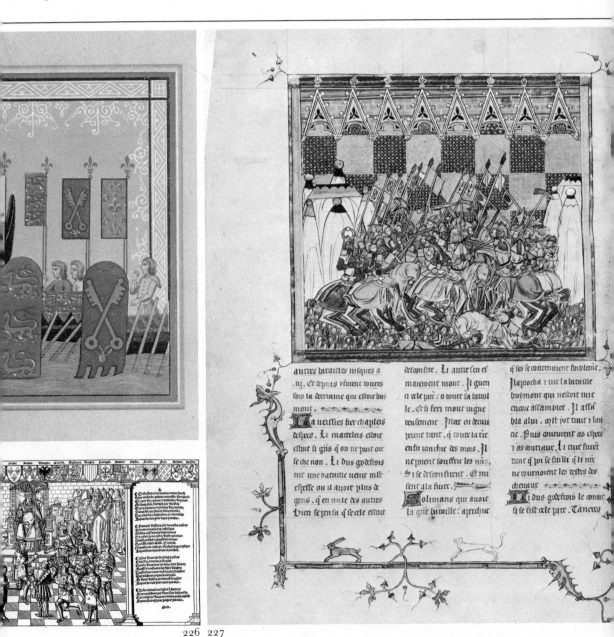

226 227

108 The siege of the city of Antioch (1098) was arduous and the flagging Crusaders' morale was saved only by the opportune "discovery" of the Holy Lance, the one that had supposedly been used to pierce Christ's side at the Crucifixion (228, 229). Even some of the leaders were doubtful about its authenticity, but morale is too precious a thing in warfare for a commander to worry how it is kept up. The siege was a classic example of this type of warfare. The Crusaders built the tower of "Malregard" to contain the sorties of the garrison. They were reinforced by troops brought up the Orontes river by Genoese ships (230). But still they could not breach the massive walls, and the town fell only because of treason on the part of some of the inhabitants. As soon as it was taken the Crusaders were themselves besieged by the Turkish relieving army. The Crusaders won a complete victory, helped partly

229

228

by desertions from the enemy army. After much wrangling, Bohemond was left as Prince of Antioch and the main army continued on to Jerusalem under the leadership of Raymond of Toulouse. The success of the final assault on the city walls was largely due to the construction of a siege tower under Raymond's command. The city was taken on 15th July, 1099 (231). For eighteen hours the Christian army slaughtered the Muslim and Jewish inhabi-

tants (232). This sack opened a new era of brutality in warfare in the Middle East. A new Christian kingdom was in the making. On the north it was protected by the county of Edessa, won by Baldwin Le Bourg. Baldwin had left the main army at Antioch to win a state for himself, and so incidentally provided an important strategic bridgehead in Arab territory.

231

230

232

In 1100 Baldwin, the best soldier and certainly the most clear-headed among the Crusaders, became King of Jerusalem. He consolidated the frontiers and, most importantly, ensured that the Crusaders had sea access for forces and supplies by winning the fine harbour of Acre (233, 234). At his death the Crusaders' adventure seemed to be political reality. Now the military problem was to defend the gains against enemies on all sides (235).

Numerous castles, like Monfort on the pilgrim route to Jerusalem, were built to consolidate the position (236). A decisive battle had been fought at Ramleh in Palestine in 1106 when the Fatimid ruler of Egypt had been defeated (237). The Arab horsemen had been scattered by a triumphant charge of the Franks. In a set battle like this, the weight of the Crusaders' cavalry was bound to tell. But to complement this they also developed a body of light horse-

233

men, the Turcopoles, who were modelled on Byzantine light cavalry. The crack troops, however, were the members of military orders, the semi-monastic Knights Templar and Knights Hospitaller (238, 239, 240). These knights were superb soldiers. Their increasing wealth from endowments made by the princes of *outre-mer* and pious laymen in Europe led them to act independently and sometimes against the general interest of the Christian states in the Holy Land. As they became acclimatized to their new land the Christians became part of it. They did not hesitate to ally with Arab states such as Damascus when it suited their interest, and often adopted aspects of Arab dress. One of the keys to their strategy was Egypt and some of the kings led expeditions there—one of which nearly captured Cairo.

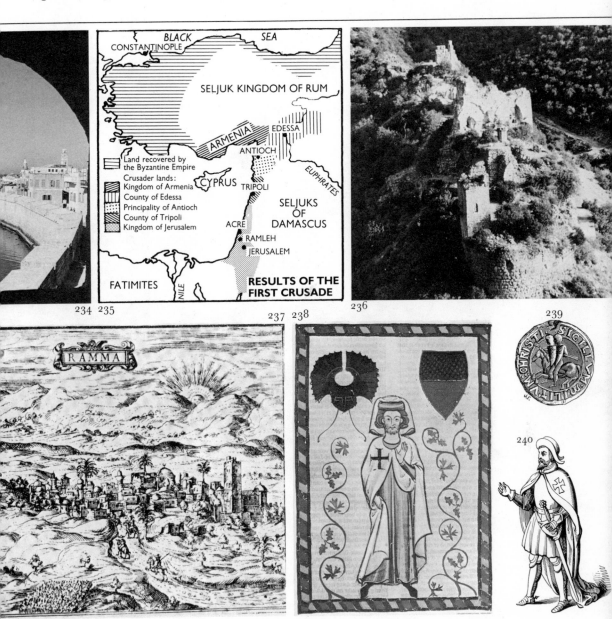

234 235 237 238 236 239 240

But Christian strategy was betrayed by self-seeking princes. Raids by the garrisons of Montreal and Kerak on the Arab caravan routes from Egypt to Damascus encouraged the Christians' enemies to unite. In 1146 Edessa was lost and then in 1187 Saladin (241) took Jerusalem, Acre and much else, razing fortifications that could not be used (242). The Third Crusade (1189–92) planned to recapture the port of Acre. King Richard I (1189–99) a master of siege warfare, took command (243 and page 56). Richard's genius as a general was control and timing. At the battle of Arsuf in Syria he held his horsemen back in the face of incessant attacks by Saracen infantry and light horse, but when he unleashed the charge the result was complete victory. It was a classic of European war style. Saladin's secretary, watching the battle, gasped in admiration. Richard won his last battle at Jaffa in August,

241

1192. The front line of his small force consisted of dismounted men-at-arms posted behind a row of tent-pegs, their shields forming a wall and their lances placed to slope upwards to impale the enemy horse. Wave after wave failed to break through. As they tired, Richard ordered his archers to the front to fire a volley and then on horseback led his men-at-arms to the attack. When his horse was shot Saladin chivalrously sent him a remount. The victory was superb, but the Crusaders could not follow it up. Richard refused even to look upon Jerusalem though other Crusaders received passes to visit the Holy Places (244). Yet he had led the chivalry of Europe to its last great victories in the Holy Land and established Christian power there for another century (245).

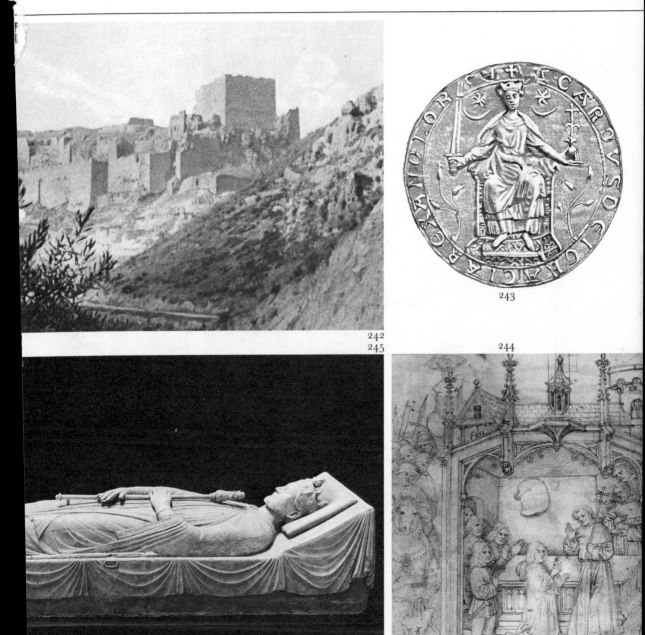

242

243

245

244

The Turks were a nomadic race from the Asian steppes, largely supporting themselves by raiding neighbouring peoples. Their victory at Manzikert in 1071 had opened the lands of Byzantine Anatolia to them. It was gradually taken over by soldier adventurers who joined the forces of frontier chiefs, the *ghazis* (warriors of the faith). In the early fourteenth century the only *ghazi* still having a frontier with the Christians was Osman. His small state was to expand under his successors Orhan and Murad (246) to become the Ottoman Empire. In the 1350s the Turks entered Europe, capturing Adrianople, and settling in large numbers. The original Turkish army had been made up of lightly armed horsemen, but Sultan Orhan reorganized it. First there was a land-based militia holding hereditary fiefs of greater or lesser value (*ziamet* and *timar*) in return for a nominal money rent and service in the army

247

246

AMURATH, I.
Third King of
The Turks.
A.º 1350.

248

249

as required. There was also the paid main force, then called the *sipahis*. The *sipahis* included armourers and gunners as well as a heavy cavalry force to whom the name was later restricted (247, 248, 249). Armed with bows, lances and sword, these were the crack horsemen. They received landed estates for life but the chief attraction was the hope of booty. The infantry consisted of the *piyade* (land-holders) and the *azabs* (recruited from the Anatolian peasants) and were armed with lance, sword and large shield (250). They were supplemented by other troops such as Moorish volunteers. The notorious *bashi-bazouks* were irregulars recruited from all over the Middle East and Europe lured by the hope of rich plunder.

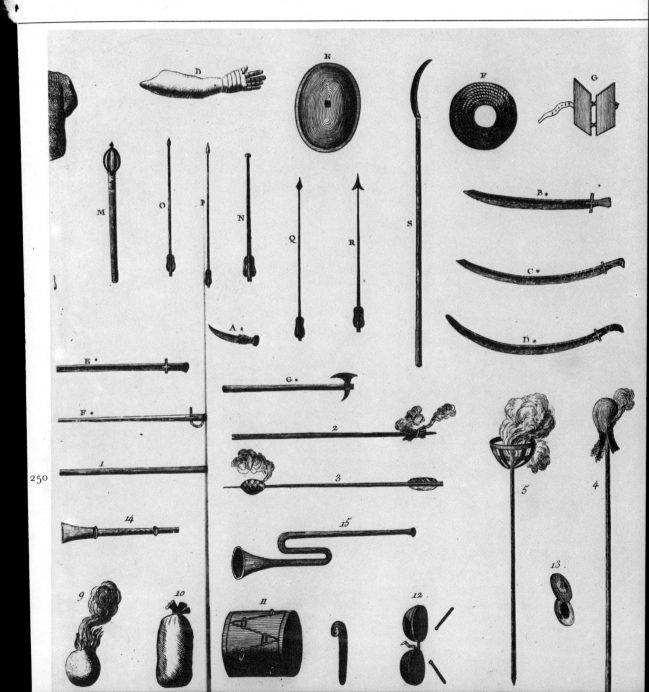

250

The best known of all the Sultan's soldiers and one of the most famous corps in military history were the Janissaries, the terror of many battles in their tall white hats and flowing robes (251). Their weapons were the bow or crossbow and the scimitar. In general they wore little or no body armour, though other Turkish troops did (252). They adopted the hand gun only in 1500 (253). Noted for their absolute discipline, the Janissaries were recruited from Christian boys indoctrinated into Islam who, as often happens with converts, were more fanatical than believers. Janissary music has become a synonym for strident martial music. The great Turkish victory over the Crusader army at Nicopolis in 1396 was won by the heavy *sipahi* cavalry led by the Sultan Bayezit himself. Against the advice of King Sigismund of Hungary (254) the Western knights insisted on charging in the grand old

251

252

253   254

feudal way. Sultan Bayezit had drawn up his army on a slope. It was covered by a line of skirmishers, easily overcome by the Westerners. Then came a row of stakes and a body of archers. Here the knights had to dismount to continue their advance and only as they reached the brow of this hill did they see the Turkish cavalry. The Sultan demanded heavy ransoms for his noble prisoners. In May, 1453, Sultan Mehmet II captured Constanti-nople (255). There were barely 7,000 male defenders against an army of 80,000. The army was equipped with the latest cannon, built under the direction of a renegade Hungarian engineer named Urban. Behind the great walls built by Theodosius centuries before the heroic defenders under their last Emperor Constantine XI (1449–53) held out for six weeks. It was the end of an epoch of Christian history.

255

For fifteen years, from 1419 to 1434, central Europe witnessed an army of peasants and gentry destroying one army after another of mounted knights sent against them by the German Emperor and the Church. The Hussites of Bohemia seemed about to repeat the successes of the Swiss, and they were defeated by their own divisions rather than by the superiority of their enemies. The Hussites took their name from Jan Hus (256). He was burned as a heretic in 1415 with the connivance of Sigismund who, as Emperor, was overlord of Bohemia. Hus's followers demanded religious reform. The extremists among them formed a fierce army of patriotic religious enthusiasts, and demanded the overthrow of established society and the return to primitive Christian communism. The Hussites established themselves in camps outside Prague to which they gave the Biblical names of Tabor and Horeb.

256

257

259

Descending from these strongholds, peasant armies drove Emperor Sigismund from the country in 1420 (257). They were led by Jan Zizka, a member of the lesser gentry and a professional soldier (258). The first success was due to the impetuous zeal of the Hussites, but then Bohemia was repeatedly invaded by the German imperial army. In the early years, equipped only with peasant weapons such as threshing flails and pitchforks, the Bohemians relied on entrenchments and defensive works to check the enemy cavalry. Yet they won great victories, like that at Kutna Hora in Bohemia in 1422. The chalice, which symbolized their demands that laymen should take the wine as well as the bread at Holy Communion, became a terrible emblem for the Catholic armies (259).

258

The Hussite general Jan Zizka died in 1424, but his genius had united two factors new to Europe which made a virtually invincible formation. In Russia Zizka had seen the *goliaigorod* or moving fortress of transport wagons which could be used as a defensive formation, or laager. The Hussites first used ordinary farm wagons, but later built stronger vehicles with grappling-hooks at each end (260). Also, Zizka made the fullest use of artillery and handguns. The Hussite laager, its wagons mounted with primitive howitzers, became an impregnable fortress. The system was perfected by Zizka's successor, Prokop the Shaven. Each wagon carried a score of men, half armed with pikes and flails posted between the wagons. The rest with bows or handguns poured a rain of missiles from gun ports in the wagon sides. They marched in five columns with the cavalry and field artillery in the

260

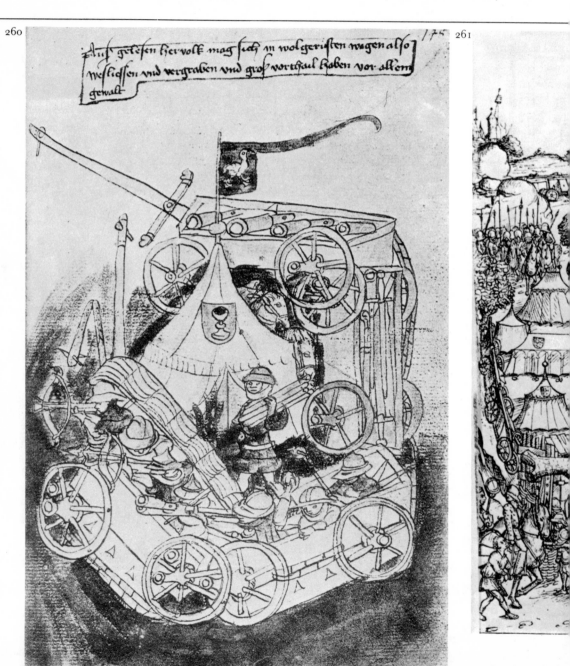

261

middle. The system relied on the skill of the highly trained drivers, who could throw their cumbersome vehicles into various combinations with a discipline that astonished contemporaries (261). The standard oblong laager could be formed so fast that the Hussites could march between the columns of a German army, set up their defence, and divide the enemy before it could attack. Soon these warriors of God began to attack by charging from the laager with such force that the enemy often fled without a fight. But the laager, designed as defence against heavy ill-disciplined cavalry, could only win against such an enemy. At the battle of Lipan (1434) Prokop's army was defeated by opposing Hussite forces who cut off the charging foot-soldiers from their wagons by a cavalry charge.

The Spanish Arab Caliphate of Cordoba was divided into military districts further subdivided into *iktas*. The *iktas* were granted to noble families in return for military service. The system probably originated in Byzantium. But soon the mercenaries, usually foreign slaves, were introduced. The Caliph Hakim I (796–822) retained a standing army of 5,000 of which 2,000 were garrisoned in the capital. On the frontiers there were establishments called *ribats* where the faithful came to make religious and military preparation for the *jihad* (holy war). Each year an expedition set out from Cordoba for the Christian north, after a ceremony in the main mosque (262). The marching column was headed and brought up by light horsemen (263). The footmen, armed with lances and small shields (264) marched with lances dragging the ground, the points forward. In battle they held off the enemy

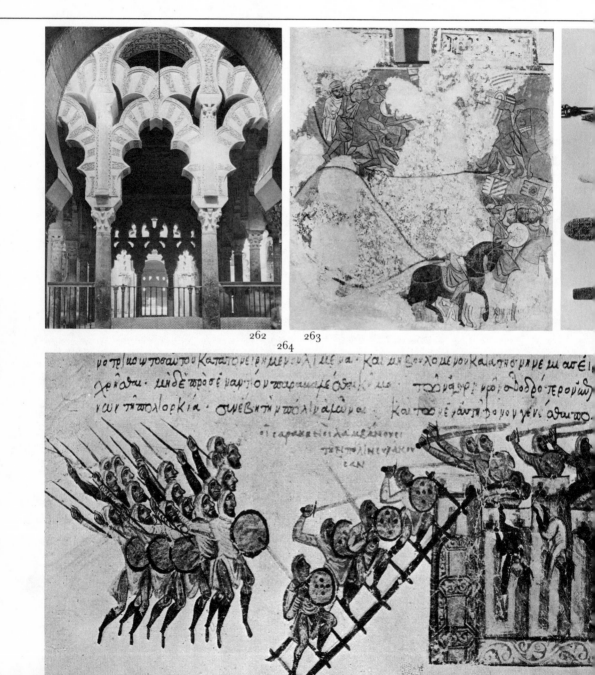

262   263

264

cavalry while the archers shot. Then the infantry opened their ranks to allow their own cavalry to charge. The Almohade Emir, Abd el Mowmin, was preceded into battle by the Koran of the Caliph Othman. And when he mounted for the day's march a hundred sheiks joined him in prayer before returning to their posts. On the march they went before him, each accoutred in gold, carrying swords and lances encrusted with ivory and silver

(265). The last great Islamic victory in Spain was at Alarcos in 1195. Alarcos had few important results and was followed, in 1212, by the crushing defeat of Las Navas de Tolosa (266). Holding a narrow pass, the Almohade army was routed by Alfonso VIII of Castile (267) who sent a division around the mountains to take them in the rear.

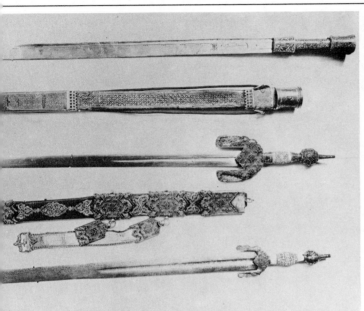

265   266

267

In the tenth century the Christian monarchs consolidated their slow reconquest of Spain by founding towns and granting lands in return for upkeep of fortifications and army service. Horsemen regularly raided Muslim lands. The hero El Cid (died 1090) gained fame against the Moorish lord of Saragossa (268). And even Spanish kings sometimes allied with the Infidel. In the twelfth century, however, Crusading enthusiasm changed things. Lisbon was captured in 1147 (269) with the help of some Englishmen going to the Second Crusade. And the Spanish military religious orders of Calatrava (270, 271), Santiago and Alcantara were founded. In the late fifteenth century Gonsalve de Cordoba (the "Great Captain") revolutionized the Spanish army. To defeat the Swiss pike phalanx he used troops with small bucklers and short swords; with these light weapons they could dart under the pikes

268

269   270

and stab the pikemen. But Gonsalve's real achievement was to combine pikes (272), arquebus (musket) men (273) and sword and buckler troops in flexible combinations to meet all eventualities. The pikemen held off a cavalry attack while the slow-loading arquebuses shot down the oncoming horsemen. The sword and bucklers were used against pikemen. As the sixteenth century passed these last were needed less. A body of cavalry was attached to each infantry division and by the 1530s the Spanish *tercio* of 3,000 men, comprising groups of specialists, had evolved. With this flexibility and specialization a new art of war was born. At the opening of the modern era of warfare, the Spaniards were lords of the field.

272

271

273

FURTHER READING

C. Blair, *European Armour* (New York, 1959; London, 1958)

H. Delbrueck, *Geschichte der Kriegskunst im Rahmen der polstuschen Geschichte*, Vol. III (Berlin, 1907)

J. G. Edwards, *Edward I's Castle Building in Wales* (New York, 1951; London, 1944)

H. R. Fedden and P. Thomson, *Crusaders' Castles* (New York, 1958; London, 1957)

G. Hindley, *Castles of Europe* (London, 1968)

M. Keen, *The Laws of War in the Later Middle Ages* (Toronto, 1965; London, 1965)

F. Lot, *L'Art militaire et les armées au moyen age* (Paris, 1949)

C. W. C. Oman, *The Art of War in the Middle Ages* (London, 1924). Shortened revised edition by John H. Beeler (New York, 1953; London, 1953)

R. R. Sellman, *Medieval English Warfare* (Toronto, 1960; London 1960)

R. C. Smail, *Crusading Warfare* (New York, 1956; London, 1956)

S. Toy, *A History of Fortification* (New York, 1955; London, 1955)

H. Treece and R. E. Oakeshott, *Fighting Men* (New York, 1965; London, 1963)

PICTURE CREDITS

INDEX